Truth

Key Concepts in Philosophy Series

Truth

Chase Wrenn

polity

First published in 2015 by Polity Press

Polity Press
65 Bridge Street
Cambridge CB2 1UR, UK

Polity Press
350 Main Street
Malden, MA 02148, USA

ISBN-13: 978-0-7456-6323-4 (hardback)
ISBN-13: 978-0-7456-6324-1 (paperback)

A catalogue record for this book is available from the British Library.

Typeset in 10.5 on 12 pt Sabon
by Toppan Best-set Premedia Limited
Printed and bound in Great Britain by T.J. International Ltd, Padstow, Cornwall

The publisher has used its best endeavors to ensure that the URLs for external websites referred to in this book are correct and active at the time of going to press. However, the publisher has no responsibility for the websites and can make no guarantee that a site will remain live or that the content is or will remain appropriate.

Every effort has been made to trace all copyright holders, but if any have been inadvertently overlooked the publisher will be pleased to include any necessary credits in any subsequent reprint or edition.

For further information on Polity, visit our website: politybooks.com

For Ron Medlin and the late Robert C. Walker,
as promised in 1992.

Contents

Preface and Acknowledgments

This book aims to provide an accessible overview of the philosophical debates concerning the metaphysics of truth. It focuses on three sets of issues. First, and most centrally, is the question of the nature of truth. What does it mean for a claim to be true, and is there anything true claims have in common that makes them true? Second is the question of objectivity. Are there claims whose truth is mind-independent, or does truth always depend on what people believe or what could be known? Third is the question of truth's value. How, if at all, is it better for beliefs to be true than false?

I have tried throughout this book to presuppose only as much background knowledge of logic and philosophy as a third- or fourth-year undergraduate would have. Consequently, I have generally avoided technical issues arising in connection with the semantic paradoxes (such as that posed by 'This sentence is false') and the formal details of alternatives to classical logic. Where necessary, discussion of those issues proceeds informally and omits many technical details. Burgess & Burgess (2011) is an excellent resource for those who are interested in how the semantic paradoxes and other issues in philosophical logic bear on the metaphysical problems discussed in this book.

The heart of this book (Chapters 4–7) surveys correspondence, epistemic, deflationist, and pluralist accounts of truth. These chapters explain what motivates the theories, as well as some of their most important advantages and disadvantages. The final, eighth chapter sets aside the pros-and-cons approach and argues for the superiority of the deflationary approach to its main rivals, correspondence and pluralist theories. My hope is that that chapter will advance the debates discussed earlier in the book and thereby give students a glimpse of how they can be carried forward.

I owe thanks to Michael Lynch for encouraging me to write this book, and to my editor, Emma Hutchinson, for her help throughout the process. The book itself has been greatly improved by fruitful discussions with a number of people, especially Michael Horton and Jeremy Kelly, whose detailed comments and criticism were invaluable. Two anonymous readers for Polity Press also provided comments that helped to make this book much better than it would have been otherwise.

Feedback from the students in my 2013 seminar on truth at the University of Alabama played a crucial role in the final revisions of this book. I am very grateful to those students, including Marissa Abrams, Mitchell Dykstra, Trevor Gant, Madaline Hargrove, Trent Moore, Patrick Norton, Matthew O'Brien, Samuel Rankin, Michael Reagan, Hunter Rodriguez, and Tiffany Simms. Thanks are also due to my research assistants, Mitchell Dykstra and Matthew O'Brien, for their excellent help in preparing the manuscript.

1
What is Truth?

It is true that the earth is closer to the sun in the northern hemisphere's winter than in the northern hemisphere's summer. It is not true that the Himalayas are older than the Appalachians. What's the difference? What does it mean for something to be true, or for it not to be? What, to be succinct, is *truth*? This book is about some of the ways philosophers have tried to answer that question.

As is often the case, answering the question requires us first to get clear about what it means. There are some common confusions about truth that can get in the way of making progress toward explaining what it is. The purpose of this chapter is to clear away some of those confusions and to set the stage for the rest of the book.

1.1   Truth and the Truth

The question, 'What is truth?' strikes some people as one of the deepest and most elusive philosophical questions. Some people seem to think it is all but unanswerable. They might think knowing what truth is would mean knowing everything there is to know, or knowing the ultimate secrets of the universe – the explanations of everything puzzling, strange, surprising, wonderful, mysterious, or confusing in the world.

Knowledge of the nature of truth then seems to be a kind of mystic wisdom that might be possible for gods and prophets, but not for us ordinary people.

Fortunately for philosophers interested in truth, that view is mistaken. It derives from a couple of different confusions. One is to confuse truth with the universe or reality as a whole. But truth is not the universe. It is a property had by the claim that chickens hatch from eggs and lacked by the claim that amphibians have fur. Explaining the nature of truth means explaining the nature of that property, not explaining the universe as a whole.

A second confusion that makes 'What is truth?' seem to require mystical insight is the idea that answering the question means knowing all the most important and fundamental things. This idea might confuse the question 'What is truth?' with the similar sounding question, 'What is the truth?'.

Ordinarily, if you want to know the truth, you want to know the truth about something in particular. You want to know whether your romantic partner is faithful, or when the train is scheduled to depart, or how the new welfare policies will affect the economy. Unless you are asking about some topic that is already philosophical, 'What is the truth?' is not usually a philosophical question.

Sometimes, though, someone might ask what the truth is, and mean something very general. Such a person wants to know the truth about everything, either by knowing all there is know, or by knowing deep principles that explain everything there is to explain. This is probably impossible. We humans are incapable of omniscience, and there probably are no deep principles that explain absolutely everything, apart from the most fundamental laws of nature. Thus it might be impossible to answer the most general version of the question 'What is the truth?'. But 'What is truth?' is a very different question. Its answer need not tell us everything there is to know, or enable us to understand everything there is to understand. All it needs to do is to explain a certain property that '2 + 2 = 4' and 'Canada is north of Mexico' have in common but 'Seven is an even number' and 'France is an island' lack.

In asking 'What is truth?', we are asking the sort of 'What is X?' question Socrates was famous for pursuing. In

Euthyphro, for example, he asks, "What is piety?" and he refuses to accept an answer that is just a list of pious acts. He wants an explanation of what makes acts pious or impious, not a list of examples. He wants to know what the nature of piety is. Likewise, when we ask what truth is, we are not interested in compiling a list of examples of true claims. We are not asking for the truth about some subject matter (apart from the truth about the nature of truth), and we are not asking for an explanation of the universe as a whole. We want to know what it means for a claim to be true or false. A good answer will explain what makes true claims true and false claims false, and it will thereby tell us about the nature of truth.

In *Metaphysics*, Aristotle says, "To say of what is not that it is, or of what is that it is not, is false, while to say of what is that is, and of what is not that it is not, is true." This may not be a complete answer to the question, 'What is truth?', but it is a start. In particular, it helps to clarify the problem. We use the adjective 'true' in many different ways. We talk about true friends and false friends. A carpenter might describe a properly aligned beam as "true." True diamonds are worth more than fakes. Elvis Costello released an album called *My Aim is True*, and the title is not nonsense. Although these notions of truth might have some family relation to what Aristotle was talking about, he was clearly concerned with something else. He was concerned with the notion of truth in the sense of accuracy, of getting it right about how things are. Asking what truth is, in this sense, is asking what it means for something to be accurate or get it right about how things are.

1.2 Truth Bearers

Before we can say much about what truth is, we need to have some idea about what sort of things are capable of being true or false, in the Aristotelian sense of getting it right or wrong about how things are. There are a lot of candidates, including sentences, propositions, utterances, statements, beliefs and theories. All of these things are "truth bearers," which means they are the sorts of things that can be true or false. They all contrast with such things as mailboxes and marbles, which are not capable of being true or false in the relevant sense. Mailboxes and marbles are not truth bearers.

Among truth bearers, some might be more fundamental than others. Take utterances and sentences, for example. A sentence is a sequence of words that satisfies certain grammatical rules. An utterance is an event consisting of someone using a sentence. For example, Jack might say, "There is water in the well on Goose Hill at 7:00 p.m. local time, October 1, 2001," and Jill might also say, "There is water in the well on Goose Hill at 7:00 p.m. local time, October 1, 2001." Those are two utterances of the same sentence. If we already had an explanation of truth and falsity for sentences, we might be able to use it to explain truth and falsity of utterances: Utterances of true sentences are true, utterances of false sentences are false, and that's all there is to it. Such an explanation treats sentences as more fundamental truth bearers than utterances.

Philosophers disagree about what the most fundamental truth bearers are. Some think sentences are the most fundamental. Once we understand what it means for a sentence to be true, they think, we will be in a position to explain what it means for any other truth bearer to be true as well. Others think propositions are the most fundamental truth bearers.

A proposition, as philosophers use the term, is a certain kind of abstract object. The general idea is that a proposition is what is said when you say something and what is believed when you believe something. If Jill says, in English, "London is pretty," and Jacques says, in French, "*Londres est jolie*," there is a sense in which they have said the same thing. If you and I both believe that water is wet, there is a sense in which we believe the same thing. And if you tell me that there are potatoes in the pantry, and I believe you, there is a sense in which what I believe is what you said. Philosophers who believe in propositions think that, in order for a person to believe or say something, there must be a thing that the person believes or says. That thing is a proposition. Those who think of propositions as the fundamental truth bearers think that other truth bearers are made true (or false) by their relationships to true (or false) propositions. A belief is true when what is believed is a true proposition, for example, and an utterance is true when what is said is a true proposition.

Philosophical debates about the fundamental truth bearers can be very complicated. Sentences and propositions are the main candidates. Philosophers who think of sentences as the fundamental truth bearers often think it is metaphysically extravagant to believe in propositions. They might think so because they do not believe in any abstract objects, including numbers, properties, and propositions. Or they might think so because those who believe in propositions have been unable to give a clearly correct explanation of their so-called identity conditions – what it takes for two sentences to express the same proposition and what it takes for them to express different propositions. Philosophers who think of propositions as the fundamental truth bearers are often doubtful that anything else, including sentences, could have the features required to serve as properly *fundamental* truth bearers, and they sometimes claim that work in the philosophy of mind and the philosophy of language relying on the idea of propositions has been too fruitful and successful to discard.

This book will mostly ignore the debate about the fundamental truth bearers. Instead of taking a side, I will use the neutral term 'claim' to refer to the fundamental truth bearers, whatever they might be. Some theories, however, are expressly designed with sentences or propositions in mind as the fundamental truth bearers. When this choice makes a difference, it will be noted.

1.3   Being True and Being Taken to be True

Some people think that, when it comes down to it, there really isn't very much truth. Maybe even nothing is true. They might say, for example, that we really can't call claims about the relative positions of the earth and sun, the molecular structure of DNA, the events of the War of the Roses, or very much else true. We can't call them true because we cannot be certain of them, and, the reasoning goes, we must be certain of something before we can call it true. Some people might even take this line of thought further. They might point out that there is always room for some doubt; we can never be 100 percent certain of anything. And, since whatever is true is 100 percent certain, there really aren't any true claims. There are only more or less probable ones.

Other people take a much more permissive view. They are impressed by the idea that it is somehow improper to call what someone else believes very deeply untrue. On this view, whatever anyone believes is true. While the first view denies that anything is true, the second allows that everything is true, so long as someone believes it.

Both views are mistaken in a variety of ways. They have more sophisticated and plausible cousins that will be discussed in Chapter 2. But it is worth pausing here long enough to note a mistake the two views have in common. Each equates *being true* with *being treated as true*. According to the first view, we are rarely or never entitled to treat anything as true, and so nothing is true. According to the second view, we are rarely or never entitled to treat what someone believes as *untrue*, and so whatever anyone believes is true.

Of course, there is a great deal of difference between being true and being treated as true, just as there is a great deal of difference between being a criminal and being treated as a criminal. For a very long time, it was not at all certain that the earth was shaped more like a sphere than a pancake. Nevertheless, during that time, the earth was shaped more like a sphere than a pancake – it was true that the earth was shaped more like a sphere than a pancake. And no matter how deeply or sincerely I believe that there is another beer in the refrigerator, my believing does not make it true that one is there.

There are two important methodological points we can extract from the difference between being true and being taken to be true. First, we cannot hope to study truth the way we might study butterflies, by amassing a large collection of specimens and examining their similarities and differences. We might be able to make some progress in that way, but we could not make very much, because we do not have a guarantee that our specimens of truth are the genuine article. I might think something is true, but I could be mistaken. To study truth, then, we need to proceed more philosophically. We need to consider some plausible accounts of what truth might be, and we need to be clear about what we want a theory of truth to explain. Then we must proceed cautiously and tentatively, in hopes of finding a theory that does the work we need it to do.

Second, the failure of the idea that being true is being taken to be true can be used to illustrate an important philosophical tool for evaluating theories of truth. The following two claims might strike you as obviously correct:

(1) If there is another beer in the refrigerator, then it is true that there is another beer in the refrigerator.
(2) If the earth is shaped more like a sphere than a pancake, then it is true that the earth is shaped more like a sphere than a pancake.

In fact, almost any instance of the pattern 'If _, then it is true that _.' is correct when we fill both blanks with the same statement in English. If truth were the same as certainty, however, those same instances of the pattern 'If _, then it is certain that _.' would be correct as well. But they are not:

(3) If there is another beer in the refrigerator, then it is certain that there is another beer in the refrigerator.
(4) If the earth is shaped more like a sphere than a pancake, then it is certain that the earth is shaped more like a sphere than a pancake.

Both those claims could easily be false, even though the similar claims involving truth are true.

Another pattern whose instances are almost always correct is 'If it is true that _, then _' (assuming we fill in the blanks with the same statement in English, of course!). Two examples are:

(5) If it is true that there is another beer in the refrigerator, then there is another beer in the refrigerator.
(6) If it is true that the earth is shaped more like a pancake than a sphere, then the earth is shaped more like a pancake than a sphere.

And if truth were the same as being believed, then the corresponding instances of 'If it is believed that _, then _' would have to be correct as well:

(7) If it is believed that there is another beer in the refrigerator, then there is another beer in the refrigerator.
(8) If it is believed that the earth is shaped more like a pancake than a sphere, then the earth is shaped more like a pancake than a sphere.

Those two claims are obviously wrong, though.

The patterns 'If _, then _ is true', 'If it is true that _, then _', and their relatives have been very important in philosophical thinking about truth from the early twentieth century onward. One of the mathematician and philosopher Alfred Tarski's most influential contributions to our understanding of truth was a requirement he proposed for any theory of truth to be acceptable. An adequate theory of truth, he said, had to imply every instance of the pattern:

(9) S is true if and only if s.

where 'S' is the name of a sentence and 's' is replaced by a translation of that sentence into the language of the theory. For example, suppose we are formulating a theory of truth in English, and the theory is supposed to apply to sentences in English. (This would violate other requirements Tarski proposed, but it is good enough for our example.) And suppose we can make a name for a sentence by putting it in quotation marks. Then, given Tarski's requirement, our theory can be adequate only if it implies such things as:

(10) 'There is another beer in the refrigerator' is true if, and only if, there is another beer in the refrigerator.
(11) 'The earth is shaped more like a sphere than a pancake' is true if, and only if, the earth is shaped more like a sphere than a pancake.
(12) 'Snow is white' is true if, and only if, snow is white.
(13) 'Grass is green' is true if, and only if, grass green.

and so on.

A "T-biconditional" is an instance of Tarski's pattern, 'S is true if, and only if, s' or a claim of the form 'It is true that _, if, and only if, _', with the two blanks filled in the same way. Although there are some problematic cases, such as 'It is true that this sentence is false if, and only if, this sentence is false', almost all the T-biconditionals are obviously true. A good theory of truth will, at the very least, be consistent with those T-biconditionals. Ideally, it will explain them. We can adopt the following principle for evaluating a theory of truth, which will be called the Equivalence Principle:

> Except for those that involve paradoxes of some sort, T-biconditionals are true. An acceptable theory of truth must accommodate or explain that fact.

Sometimes this book will refer to "the Equivalence Schema." The Equivalence Schema is the pattern the T-biconditionals fit, either 'It is true that _ if, and only if, _' or 'S is true if, and only if, s.'

1.4 What Lies Ahead

The following two chapters consider a pair of problems that are closely tied to the question 'What is truth?' One is the problem of objectivity. Are there claims that are objectively, mind-independently true, or does truth depend in some way on what we think or what we could think? The other is the problem of the value of truth. In what sense are true beliefs or assertions "better" than false ones? Just as a good theory of truth will satisfy the Equivalence Principle, a good theory of truth would also provide a good understanding of objectivity and explain the value of truth. The various approaches to explaining the nature of truth that Chapters 4 through 7 explore have different commitments with respect to objectivity and value, and one way of evaluating them is to consider what those commitments are.

Further Reading

Several of Plato's dialogues deal with the difference between explaining the nature of something and listing examples. Among them are *Euthyphro*, *Meno*, and the *Republic*, which also contains a great deal of interesting discussion of the relationship of truth to knowledge.

Aristotle's views on truth are scattered through several of his works, especially the *Metaphysics* and the *Posterior Analytics*. In *Metaphysics* Book IV (Γ), Chapter 8, Aristotle argues against the views that nothing is true and that everything is true on the grounds that they are self-defeating: If nothing is true, then neither is the doctrine that nothing is true; and if everything is true, then so is the doctrine that not everything is true.

Wolfgang Künne's book, *Conceptions of Truth* (2003), includes excellent discussions of a wide range of issues, including the issue of fundamental truth bearers in its fifth chapter. The roots of the modern conception of a proposition lie in Gottlob Frege's important essay, "The Thought" (1956). The second chapter of W. V. Quine's classic, *Word and Object* (1960), argues that there is usually not a determinate fact of the matter what a person's utterances mean, which would imply that there is no determinate fact of the matter whether two people have said the same thing or expressed the same proposition. A pair of papers by Hartry Field, "Mental Representation" and "Deflationist Theories of Meaning and Content," make the case for dispensing with propositions in our understanding of belief and truth. They are both reprinted in the collection, *Truth and the Absence of Fact* (Field 2001).

Alfred Tarski's "The Semantic Conception of Truth and the Foundations of Semantics" (1944) both sets out the requirement that a good theory of truth should imply the T-biconditionals and contains a treatment of the logic of the expression '_ is true' that has been absolutely central to future logical work on truth and the paradoxes of truth (such as the paradox posed by the sentence, 'This sentence is false').

2
Objectivity

People sometimes wonder about the nature of truth because they are interested in the question whether anything is "objectively" true. Does the truth depend on what people, or the right people, believe? Or are there some claims that are true regardless of what anyone thinks? One idea of an "objective" truth is the idea of a claim whose truth or falsehood does not depend on what anyone believes.

A second set of questions also falls under the heading of objectivity. Those questions concern the relationship between truth and knowledge. Sometimes we can tell whether a claim is true or false, and sometimes it is impossible for us to know one way or the other. If there is no way to *tell* whether a claim is true or false, can it even *be* true or false? One idea of "objective" truth is the idea that the truth of a claim does not depend on whether or not we could know it. There could be claims that are true but unknowable. According to some philosophers, though, the idea of an unknowable truth is nonsense. On their view, if it is impossible to know whether something is the case, then there simply is no fact of the matter either way. These philosophers thus think of the limits of possible knowledge as the limits of truth and, in that sense, the limits of reality

This chapter concerns the three-way debate over objectivity. On one side is *realism*, the view that there are some claims whose truth does not depend on their being believed by anyone or even on the possibility of anyone's knowing them. On another side is *relativism*, the view that the truth is always a matter of opinion, in the sense that the truth of any claim always depends on who believes it. The third contender is *anti-realism*, the view that part of what makes a claim true is the fact that we can know it, and so claims we cannot know to be true or false cannot be true or false. Each view presents a different picture of how the world is, and each has its own advantages and disadvantages. This chapter discusses those advantages and disadvantages, with the upshot that a mild form of realism is the most plausible of these views.

2.1 Three Pictures of Reality

Realism, anti-realism, and relativism present different views of the world and its relationship to our minds. Realists take the commonsense view that there is a world "out there," and the facts are as they are irrespective of what anyone thinks about them. There are some claims that would be true even if no one believed them, or false even if everyone did. Moreover, although we may be able to acquire some knowledge about the mind-independent world, claims are ordinarily knowable because they are true, not true because they are knowable. What makes a claim true need not have anything to do with the possibility of knowing it. Realists might disagree with each other about which parts of reality are mind-independent, but they agree that *something* is.

Astrophysicists say parts of the universe more than about 62 billion light years away are too distant for any information from there to reach us – ever (Gott et al. 2005). Consider the claim (whose truth we could not possibly know) that there are an odd number of water molecules exactly 63 billion light years from Earth. A realist is apt to say that, regardless of whether anyone believes or disbelieves that claim, and despite the fact that we have no way of knowing one way or the other, the claim is either true or false. Either there are an odd number of water molecules 63 billion miles away, or there are not.

Relativists think of the world as made up, like a story. Truth and falsehood depend on what people believe. And just as there is no such thing as absolute "to the leftness," but only being to the left *of something*, there is no such thing as absolute truth, only truth *for someone*. A table might be to the left of the window but not of the stove, and a claim might be true for one person but false for another. Belief is what makes the difference. On the relativist view, what makes a claim true for someone is that they believe it, and what makes it false for someone is that they disbelieve it.

Suppose Jill has told a joke. Maybe some people think it is funny and some people think it isn't. It's very tempting to think the joke is funny for those who think it is, but it isn't funny for those think it isn't. It's also tempting to think that is all there is to it. There is no underlying fact about whether the joke is "really" funny or not, because part of what it means for something to *be* funny is for people to *think* it's funny. Relativists think all claims are like the claim that Jill's joke is funny. Not only the truth about funniness, but *all* truth depends on what people believe, and it is always *someone's* truth. What a person believes is true for her; what she disbelieves is false for her; and where she has no opinion, there is neither truth nor falsehood.

Anti-realists do not think truth depends on belief, and they do not think that all truth is someone's truth. But they do think truth is mind-dependent in another way. According to anti-realists, a claim cannot be true unless it is possible to *find out* or *know* it is true. Likewise, a claim cannot be false unless it is possible to *find out* or *know* it is false. If there is no way to know that a claim is true, anti-realists think, then that claim must not be true – it must either be false or have no truth value at all. On the anti-realist view, the concepts of truth and knowability are tightly linked because part of what it means for a claim to be true is that there is a way we could find out that it's true. This makes truth mind-dependent because the limits of possible knowledge are also the limits of reality. If there is no way to find out whether there are an even or odd number of water molecules exactly 63 billion light years from earth, then there is no fact of the matter about it. It's neither true nor false that there is an even number, and it's neither true nor false that there is an odd number. Instead, the question represents a gap in reality.

There are thus two big questions to be addressed in the debate among realists, relativists, and anti-realists. First, is anything true irrespective of what anyone believes? If so, then relativism is incorrect. Second, is there anything that is true even though there is no way, in principle, for anyone to know that it is? If so, then anti-realism is incorrect.

2.2 Realism

The realist picture of reality draws on two important aspects of our experience. First, we sometimes find that we have mistakenly believed something that was not true. Second, we sometimes discover truths we were unaware of before. These experiences allow us to distinguish between how things really are and what we happen to believe. A natural way to make that distinction is to think of the world as "out there" and independent of us. The world is a collection of objects or facts that are as they are regardless of what we think, and even regardless of what we *could* believe or know.

Consider, for example, the claim that the earth is shaped more like a sphere than a pancake. People used to disbelieve that claim, but they later discovered that they were mistaken. They discovered that things were not as they thought they were. But what if there had been no way for anyone to know the shape of the earth? What if no intelligent life had ever existed in the universe? Still, we tend to think, the earth would have been shaped more like a sphere than a pancake. The shape of the earth is supposed to be exactly the sort of thing that is indifferent to what we happen to believe, or even to what it is possible to know.

One of the greatest appeals of realism is its explanatory power. Realism explains why it is possible for beliefs to be mistaken. For example, it is possible for a belief about the shape of the earth to be mistaken because the shape of the earth does not depend on what anyone thinks about it. Realism also provides a way to make sense of what happens when we discover something new. There are facts that are out there, independent of us, that we have not yet come to know. Discoveries happen when we find a way to know them.

But realism goes further than that. Not only does it say there are claims whose truth does not depend on our believing them, but it says there are claims whose truth does not depend on the possibility that we could know them. Why should we think there are such facts?

One reason applies what we already know about the world. What makes it true that the earth is round, for example, appears to be something about the earth itself, not its relationship to intelligent life. After all, it was true long before there were any intelligent beings to know it, and it would have been true even if those intelligent beings had never existed. Given what we know about the world, then, there seem to be some claims whose truth does not require the possibility of their being known.

Another reason has to do with the fact that there are some claims whose truth or falsity we cannot know. Consider the claim that the last dinosaur chipped a tooth ten minutes before dying. We have no way of finding out whether that claim is true or false. However, it is natural to suppose that the dinosaur either *did* or *did not* chip a tooth ten minutes before dying. Either way, then, there is something that is true but impossible to know.

The realist conception of the world might seem appealing to common sense, but it does face some difficulties. One objection to realism is that, if there were any objectively true claims, it would be impossible to know whether those claims were true or false. According to this objection, realism makes knowledge of the mind-independent world impossible. The view that such knowledge is impossible is called "skepticism," and this objection raises the problem of skepticism for realism.

Why think realism entails skepticism? The idea is that all our knowledge ultimately derives from how things seem to us, and from no other source. "How things seem" includes our perceptual experiences, and it may also include so-called "intellectual seemings," which occur when you think about a claim and it strikes you as true or as false, regardless of your sensory experiences. For example, think about the claim that murder is wrong and the claim that $1 + 1 = 11$. The former claim probably *seems true* to you, and the latter probably *seems false*. Those are intellectual seemings.

Given realism, though, how the world *is* could be radically different from how it seems to be. A classic example in this vein is René Descartes' (1641) thought experiment involving a deceptive demon. We have no way to rule out the possibility we are the victims of a demon who has arranged for everything to seem to us as it does, even though the physical world does not exist at all. In that case, all our beliefs about the external world would be false. It would seem to us that there are tables and chairs, that there used to be dinosaurs, that objects in motion tend to stay in motion, and even that there are infinitely many prime numbers, but all those appearances are due to the demon's deceptions. Things could seem that way without any of those claims being true.

According to this objection to realism, if how things are is independent of how they seem, demon-like deception is possible. We have no way to rule it out. And since we have no way to rule it out, we cannot know whether the external world exists or, instead, is all an illusion. We cannot really know anything about the external world unless we can rule out such possibilities, and so, the objection goes, realism entails skepticism.

Realists have responded to the skeptical problem in several ways. According to Descartes, we can know that God exists, and this guarantees that how things seem is a reliable guide to how they mind-independently are. After all, God is perfectly good, and a perfectly good God would not allow us to be radically misled by how things seem. Descartes' solution does not work, though. The existence of God is precisely the sort of thing realists think of as mind-independent, and its seeming that God exists is no guarantee that he really does. Even if God didn't exist, the demon could make it seem as though he did.

Another historically important response has been to simply accept it. David Hume (1739; 1777), for example, held that all our knowledge is just an elaboration of how things seem to us. We have, on his view, no way of knowing anything beyond the appearances, and no justification for believing there is or is not anything beyond how things seem to us. We cannot help but believe there is a mind independent world, but there is no rational basis for that belief.

Immanuel Kant (1781; 1783) took an approach somewhat different from Hume's. Kant argued that experience would be impossible unless there were a mind-independent reality, whose truths do not depend on how things seem to anyone. However, he also thought we could have no detailed knowledge of that world, apart from our knowledge that it exists. On Kant's view, there are two worlds. One is the real and unknowable world of "things in themselves," and the other is the world of appearances. Our knowledge is confined to the world of appearances.

Contemporary philosophers tend to take a different approach. They point out that the skeptical problem requires two key presuppositions. First is the realist presupposition that how things are does not depend on how they seem. Second, though, is the presupposition that knowledge requires us to rule out all possibilities of error. Contemporary philosophers typically think this second presupposition is mistaken. Knowing something requires one to have *good enough* evidence that it is true, but evidence can be good enough without ruling out such arcane possibilities as that we are victims of Descartes' demon. The realist who takes this view of knowledge can then agree that we are not guaranteed our beliefs about the mind-independent world are true, but our evidence can be good enough for knowledge anyway.

2.3 Relativism

According to relativists, there is no such thing as how the world really is, apart from what people believe. Truth is relative to people and their beliefs, and what is true for one person might not be true for someone else. There are many different kinds of relativism. According to *subjectivism*, truth is relative to individuals. What is true for a given person is what that person believes, and what is false for her is what she disbelieves. Other varieties of relativism, which we'll simply call "consensus relativism," hold that truth is relative to groups of people. What a group of people believes is true for that group, and what the group disbelieves is false for it. On most versions of consensus relativism, though, truth is not relative to just any arbitrary group. Rather, only certain kinds of groups matter. For example, some consensus relativists think truth is relative to cultures, to races, to religions, to classes, to genders, to politically powerful groups, or to some combination of them.

We have already seen, in Chapter 1, why truth cannot be the same thing as belief. Not everything believed is true, and not everything true is actually believed by anyone. This also spells trouble for relativism.

Subjectivism is implausible for several reasons. One of the most significant of them is that, if it were correct, then no one would ever be mistaken about anything. If all it takes for a claim to be true for a person is for her to believe it, then whatever she believes is true for her. She can't be wrong. But people are mistaken about things all the time. People make mistakes about how much money is in their bank account, about what time a meeting has been scheduled, about whether $517 \times 3 = 1,531$, and many other things. We cannot make things true by believing them. This is not just a matter of one person's believing something that someone else disbelieves. Rather, it is a common and important part of the human experience that we often find out that some things we have believed are not true after all. That would be impossible given subjectivism.

At first blush, consensus relativism might seem to avoid that problem. It is possible for an individual to believe something that a group does not, and even for an individual to disagree with a group to which he or she belongs. If whatever a group believes is true for that group, then anyone who disagrees with the group is mistaken, relative to that group. So, given consensus relativism, there is a way in which individuals can have mistaken beliefs, even though truth and falsehood depend on what groups of people believe.

Nevertheless, consensus relativism faces a version of the same problem as subjectivism, transposed into a different key. Even if an individual's belief can be mistaken relative to a given group, consensus relativism leaves no room for *groups* to have false beliefs. For example, suppose truth is relative to cultures. Then, if a culture believes the earth is flat, then it is true for that culture that the earth is flat. The culture cannot be mistaken about the shape of the earth, and that means it is impossible for them to *discover* that they have been mistaken about the shape of the earth. If a different group believes that the earth is round, then it simply turns out that the earth is flat for one group and round for the other, and that's all there is to it. There is, on consensus relativism, no deeper fact of the matter about the shape of the earth, apart from what different groups think about it.

Another set of problems for relativism arises from the fact that the view is self-undermining in at least two ways. One of them derives from an objection that Plato and Aristotle each raised to the view of the ancient relativist, Protagoras, who is known for saying "Man is the measure of all things, of things that are that they are, and of things that are not that they are not."

Here is how the objection goes. Let's call the denial of relativism "absolutism." According to absolutism, there are some claims whose truth does not depend on anyone believing them. Realism is one kind of absolutism. Now suppose for the sake of argument that relativism is true. Either it is true only for relativists, or it is true regardless of what anyone believes about it. If it is true regardless of what anyone believes about it, then there is a claim whose truth does not depend on anyone believing it. In that case, absolutism is true after all, and relativism is false. On the other hand, if relativism is only true for relativists, then relativism is false for absolutists and absolutism is true for absolutists. Either way, absolutism turns out to be true. This argument is sometimes called the "peritrope," which comes from Greek words that mean "turning the table," because it shows how the assumption of relativism can be used to argue *against* relativism.

There is another interesting and subtle response to relativism. The idea is that, if relativism were true, there would be no facts of the matter about what anyone believed. Consequently, nothing could even be true or false *for a person* (or group). Here is how it works. Suppose Alice believes that Bob believes there is milk in the refrigerator. And suppose that Bob believes that Bob does not believe there is milk in the refrigerator. Thus, it is true for Alice that it is true for Bob that there is milk in the refrigerator. But it is false for Bob that it is true for Bob that there is milk in the refrigerator. So, is it true or false for Bob that there is milk in the refrigerator? Given relativism, there is no single correct answer. If Bob and Alice disagree about what is true for Bob, then what is true for Bob for Alice is different from what is true for Bob for Bob, and nothing is just plain true for Bob!

The above objection does not depend on anything in particular about subjectivism. We could replace Alice and Bob's names with the names of groups, and the same problem would arise. It so happens that this problem for relativism might be especially important in the contemporary world of globalization.

Here is a troubling application. There are radicals in the United States who believe that Muslims believe they are commanded by God to kill anyone who isn't a Muslim. Almost all Muslims believe that that is no part of Islam. They think that Muslims do *not* believe they have such a commandment from God. But given relativism, the radicals in the United States cannot be wrong. They cannot be wrong about what Muslims believe, even if the *Muslims* disagree with them about what their religion teaches. It would turn out to be true for the radicals that Muslims believe they are commanded by God to kill non-Muslims, and false for the Muslims that they believe they are commanded by God to kill non-Muslims.

Cases like this show that relativism is not just an inconsequential metaphysical error, but a potentially disastrous kind of mistake. The radicals who believe that Muslims think they are commanded to kill non-Muslims use this idea to justify doing various horrible things to Muslims, from denying them the right to build mosques to attacking them physically and even torturing or killing them. One of the most important means of opposing such mistreatment is to point out that it is motivated by a *false* view of what Muslims in fact believe. Unfortunately, relativism makes that impossible. Assuming relativism, no matter what Muslims think they believe, it is true for the radicals that Muslims believe whatever the radicals think they believe.

Given the serious problems for the view, one might wonder why anyone would be attracted to relativism in the first place. Often, people accept relativism because they commit the error of overgeneralizing. There are some matters about which truth might be relative to what people believe. For example, whether it is true or not that a joke is funny might depend on whether people think it is funny. And maybe there is no absolute fact of the matter about funniness. For those who think a joke is funny, it is true that it is funny. And for those who do not, it is not. It is a mistake, though, to think that the truth of *all* claims is relative just because the truth of some claims seems to be.

Another line of thought in favor of relativism is this:

(1) There is no way to tell the difference between what is true and what you happen to believe or what seems true from your particular perspective.

(2) If there is no way to tell the difference between what is true and what you happen to believe or what seems true from your particular perspective, then there *is* no difference between what is true and what you happen to believe or what seems true from your particular perspective.

(3) And if there is no such difference, truth is relative to what people believe.

(4) Therefore, truth is relative to what people believe.

Though the argument is formally valid, its first two premises are seriously problematic. The first premise is ambiguous. It could mean either of these two things:

(1a) If you believe something or it seems true from your perspective, there is no way to *ever* tell the difference between what you believe and what is true.

(1b) If you believe something or it seems true from your perspective at a given moment, there is no way *at that moment* to tell the difference between what you believe and what is true.

On interpretation (1a), the premise is obviously false. We often discover that things we previously believed were not true, even though they seemed true before. That means that we can and do tell the difference between what is true and what we happen to have believed or what seemed true to us earlier. Likewise, in the future we might discover that some-thing we now believe is not true. That too means we can, eventually, tell the difference between at least some of what we believe and what is true.

So, if the argument is to have any hope at all, we must see the first premise as meaning (1b). But then, for the argument to be valid, the second premise must mean this:

(2b) If there is no way to tell, at any given moment, the difference between what is true at that moment and what you happen to believe or what seems true from your particular perspective at that moment, then there *is* no difference between what is true at that moment and what you happen to believe or what seems true from your particular perspective at that moment.

But now this premise is implausible. Again, it is crucial that we have firsthand experience of having been mistaken. Even if we grant that we cannot, at a particular moment, tell the difference between what is true and what we happen to believe, we can still be mistaken about how things are. Maybe there is no way for me to tell the difference, *at this very instant*, between its being true that my house is on fire and my believing falsely that my house is on fire. Nevertheless, there is all the difference in the world between my *believing*, at a certain time, that the house is on fire and its actually *being* on fire at that time. That is why I am so relieved when, later, I find out that my house was not on fire when I thought it was (or any other time).

People have offered other arguments for relativism. Some argue for relativism from the fact that we can only know how things seem to us, not how they really are. But that premise does not actually support relativism. Instead, it merely implies a form of skepticism: *if* there is a way things are apart from how they seem, then we cannot know much about it. Others argue for relativism on the grounds that that whatever we take to be "the truth" is always what someone believes or what someone wants us to believe. But again, relativism does not follow from that premise unless we also suppose that nothing can be true unless someone thinks it is true. Not only does that beg the question, but it is clearly false. If nothing could be true unless someone thought it was, there could never be any undiscovered truths. It would be impossible to discover that something no one believed before is true, and people would already believe everything true. Relativism is simply not a plausible alternative to realism.

2.4 Anti-Realism

Often, we can tell whether a claim is true or false. We can look in the refrigerator to see whether 'There is milk in the refrigerator' is true or false. We can do calculations to find out whether '4,517 is a prime number' is true or false. There are some claims, though, whose truth value we have no way, in principle, to figure out. Philosophers might disagree about some of the particular cases, but here are some likely examples:

(5) Paul Giamatti is bald.
(6) There is an odd number of water molecules exactly 63 billion light years from earth.
(7) The last dinosaur died on a Wednesday.
(8) There is no set with more members than the set of integers but fewer members than the set of real numbers.

Example (5) involves a vague term, 'bald'. Paul Giamatti certainly has less hair than Daniel Radcliffe, but he has more than Vin Diesel. So, is he bald or not? Even if we had a complete census of all the hairs on Paul Giamatti's head and their locations, we might be unable to settle the question. There seems to be no way of knowing whether it is true or false that Paul Giamatti is bald.

Examples (6) and (7) concern matters that are too far away in time or space for anyone to be able to find out. Our best science tells us that there is no way to get any information from more than about 62 billion light years away, but the universe is much larger than that. There is thus no way, in principle, for us to know whether (6) is true or false. And the last dinosaur died so long ago that there is nothing we could do to find out the exact date of its death, in order to check whether that day was a Wednesday or not.

Example (8) is known as the Continuum Hypothesis. The mathematician Kurt Gödel showed that there is no way to prove or disprove it from the usual axioms of set theory. Gödel also proved that, in any consistent mathematical system powerful enough to state all the mathematical truths, there will always be some sentences that can be neither proven nor disproven.

On the realist conception of truth, the impossibility of *knowing* whether a claim is true makes no difference to whether it *is* true. Sometimes, it is impossible to know whether a claim is true because there is simply no fact of the matter. Maybe that is what happens with vagueness. We cannot know whether it is true or false that Paul Giamatti is bald because there is no fact of the matter as to whether he is bald, and where there is no fact of the matter, there can be no truth. According to realism, though, there are some facts that do not answer to us. Maybe it's true that the last dinosaur died on a Wednesday, and maybe it's false, but either way the question has nothing to do with whether it is possible, even in principle, for anyone to know which.

Anti-realists think there is a way in which the facts answer to us. They do not agree with relativists that truth is a matter of being believed by the right people. Instead, they think, when there is no way for us to find out whether a sentence is true or false, there is no fact of the matter. Such sentences are not true, and they are not false either. Unless we have a way of finding out one way or the other, there is no fact of the matter as to whether Paul Giamatti is bald, whether there is an even number of water molecules exactly 63 billion light years from earth, whether the last dinosaur died on a Wednesday, or whether there is a set larger than the set of integers but smaller than the set of real numbers.

Realism reflects the intuition that the world is out there, independent of us, and, if we're lucky, we can investigate it and gain some knowledge of how things are. Anti-realists are motivated by a different set of considerations. They start by asking about the content of our concept of truth. Consider a couple of claims whose truth or falsity we *could* know, such as 'There is milk in the refrigerator' and '4,517 is a prime number'. Suppose it is true that there is milk in the refrigerator. What is it, exactly, that you are supposing? It seems that, if we imagine the claim is true, we are imagining that the world is such that, for example, someone who walked to the refrigerator and opened it would find a nonempty milk carton. Someone who poured out the carton's contents would find they tasted and smelled and looked like milk. Chemical analyses of those contents would yield results as expected of milk. An examination of the history of the carton and its contents would lead one eventually to find it was filled with a liquid extracted from the udders of cows. And so on. When you imagine that the claim is true, you are imagining the various ways you could *find out* it is true there is milk in the refrigerator.

Now suppose it is true that 4,517 is a prime number. A prime number is one that is evenly divisible only by itself and 1. To suppose that 4,517 is prime is to suppose that, were one to check all the numbers between 1 and 4,517, one would find that none of them divides into 4,517 evenly. There seems to be no difference between supposing it is true that 4,517 is prime and supposing it is possible to prove that 4,517 is prime.

Take a claim whose truth or falsity we cannot find out. As anti-realists see it, all there is to supposing the claim is true is imagining what it would be like to find out it is true. And all there is to supposing the claim is false is imagining what it would be like to find out that its negation (e.g., 'Paul Giamatti is not bald', 'The last dinosaur did not die on a Wednesday', etc.) is true. But if there is no way to find out that a claim is true, then we are not imagining *anything* if we imagine that it is true. There is no way to prove or disprove the Continuum Hypothesis (from the ordinary axioms of set theory), so there is nothing for me to suppose if I suppose it is true or false.

According to anti-realists, there is no difference between supposing a claim is true and supposing it is possible, in principle, to find out that the claim is true. Additionally, they think, if there is no difference between what we are supposing in those two cases, then there is no difference between a claim's *being* true and its being possible to find out that it's true. The very concept of truth, on their view, is the concept of knowability, and so anything true is, in principle, knowable.

We can express the line of thought just outlined in the following argument:

(9) To suppose that a claim is true is to imagine what would be involved in finding out that it is true, i.e., coming to know it.

(10) All that is involved in a claim's *being* true is what we imagine when we suppose it *is* true.

(11) Therefore, for a claim to be true is for it to be knowable.

Of course, if being true just is being knowable, then it follows that there can be no unknowable truths.

How could realists respond to this argument? They might reject either premise. Against (9), they could contend that there is a difference between supposing a claim is true and imagining finding out it is true. We can imagine, for example, that no intelligent life had ever arisen in the universe. Much of the world would be pretty much as it is now. There would be stars and planets, hydrogen atoms and dark matter, even if no one ever existed to find out about them. And, since we are imagining a universe without intelligent life, we must not be imagining *finding out* any of those things. So, it seems, imagining those things are true and imagining finding out they true are two different things after all. An anti-realist is likely to reply, however, that there is something incoherent about imagining what the universe would be like if we had never existed to find out about it. What are we imagining when we do that? How could we imagine what the world would be like without imagining someone *for whom* it would be like that?

Realists could also reject (10), the second premise of the argument. They could contend that what is involved in a claim's being true is not the same as what we imagine when we imagine it is true. We are all aware that there are things we do not know. That is a lesson we learn in the process of learning new things, and in the process of rooting out our previously mistaken beliefs. There are unknown truths, and we have a clear idea what it means for something to be an unknown truth. That could be enough to give us the idea that some aspects of the world are as they are, even without our finding out about them. Dinosaurs did not spring into existence when their fossils were first discovered. They lived and died millions of years before us, and that would have been so even if we never found out about them. But once we understand that there are some things that would have been so even if we never found out about them, it seems easy to suppose that there are things that are so even though we *cannot* find out about them. After all, we do know that the last dinosaur died on some day or other, because we know that the dinosaurs are extinct. But if the last dinosaur died on some day or other, then it must be true that it died on a Sunday, Monday, Tuesday, Wednesday, Thursday, Friday, or Saturday. A realist will point out how little sense it makes to think both that, for each day of the week, it is neither true nor false that the last dinosaur died on that day, and also that it is true that the last dinosaur died on some day or other, even if we can't know which.

Anti-realism thus seems to require adjustments to classical logic. In classical logic, a statement of the form *Either A or B* is true only if either *A* is true or *B* is true. But take the case of the last dinosaur. We can and do know that it died on some day or other, so we can and do know:

(12)   Either the last dinosaur died on a Sunday, or a Monday, or a Tuesday, or a Wednesday, or a Thursday, or a Friday, or a Saturday.

However, it may be unknowable *which* day the last dinosaur died. That would mean that none of the following claims are knowable, and an anti-realist might have to hold that all of them are neither true nor false:

(Su)   The last dinosaur died on a Sunday.
(M)   The last dinosaur died on a Monday.
       etc. through
(Sa)   The last dinosaur died on a Saturday.

Given classical logic, (12) can't be true unless one of (Su) through (Sa) is true. But (12) can be knowable even if (Su) through (Sa) aren't. So, an anti-realist may need to adopt a logic that could allow (12) to be true even though (Su) through (Sa) are each neither true nor false. Realists, naturally, are apt to think that giving up anti-realism is a better option than giving up classical logic.

Much of the debate between realists and anti-realists involves one side pointing out something that seems nonsensical in the other side's view. Anti-realists think we simply have no concept of a claim's being true even though there is no way of finding out that it is, and so anyone who thinks an unknowable sentence is true or false (but we know not which) is simply deluding himself. Realists think it is nonsense to suppose reality has the sort of gaps anti-realists are committed to, and that it's equally incoherent to suppose a sentence like 'The last dinosaur died on some day or other' could be true even though there is no particular day on which the last dinosaur died.

A very serious problem for anti-realism was discovered by Alonzo Church and reported in a paper of Frederic Fitch's. Church brought the problem to Fitch's attention anonymously, and so it has been known as "Fitch's Paradox" until recently, when it has come to be called "The Paradox of Knowability." The problem is just this: The claim that every truth is know*able* seems to have the very surprising implication that every truth is, in fact *known*!

The reasoning behind the Paradox of Knowability can be a little bit hard to follow. It depends on a couple of principles that are worth setting out before going through the argument. First is the *Factivity of Knowledge*:

> *Factivity of Knowledge:* For any claim, *p*, if it is known that *p*, then *p*.

Informally speaking, the idea is that you can't know what isn't so. If there isn't any milk in the refrigerator, it can't be known that there is milk in the refrigerator. And if anyone knows that there is milk in the refrigerator, then there *is* milk in the refrigerator.

The second principle is often called *Single Premise Closure* (the reasons for that name are not important for our purposes):

Single Premise Closure: If a conjunction, '*p* and *q*', is known, then *p* is known and *q* is known.

For example, if it is known that Jack and Jill went up the hill, then it is known that Jack went up the hill, and it is known that Jill went up the hill. If it is known that snow is white and grass is green, then it is known that snow is white, and it is known that grass is green. The general idea is that knowing a conjunction of two claims entails knowing each of those claims separately as well.

Here is the reasoning behind the paradox. To show that, given anti-realism, every truth is known, we will try to show that the opposite cannot be true. That is, we will try to show that anti-realism is inconsistent with the claim that there is a claim that is true but not known. Let *p* be a claim that is true but unknown. That is, suppose:

(13) The following is true: *p* is true and *p* is not known.

Now, since anti-realism is the view that whatever is true is knowable, (13) and anti-realism imply:

(14) The following is possible: Someone knows that both (a) *p* is true and (b) *p* is not known.

(14) says, essentially, that if something is an unknown truth, then it is knowable that it is an unknown truth. The problem arises because (14) and Single Premise Closure entail:

(15) The following is possible: Someone knows that *p* is true, and someone knows that no one knows that *p* is true.

Now, thanks to the Factivity of Knowledge, if anyone knows that no one knows that *p* is true, then no one knows that *p* is true. So, (15) entails that a contradiction is possible:

(16) The following is possible: Someone knows that *p* is true, and no one knows that *p* is true.

Contradictions are not possible, so something must have gone wrong. The Factivity of Knowledge and Single Premise Closure seem harmless. The trouble must then arise either from anti-realism or from the assumption that there is an unknown truth. So, if we accept anti-realism, we seem to be committed to rejecting the assumption that there is an unknown truth. Not only are all true claims know*able*, they are *known*!

The Paradox of Knowability might not refute anti-realism decisively, but it does highlight a cost that anti-realists must pay. Anti-realists are already committed to the idea that some sentences, which otherwise appear to be perfectly in order, are neither true nor false. All by itself, that commits anti-realists to rejecting the classical logical principle of bivalence, which says that every claim is either true or false. The Paradox of Knowability further requires the anti-realist to choose among the following options, none of which seems particularly attractive:

- Deny the Factivity of Knowledge or Single Premise Closure.
- Deny the existence of unknown truths.
- Adopt a non-classical logic that not only violates the principle of bivalence, but in which 'There are no unknown truths' is not equivalent to 'All truths are known.'

2.5   Objectivity and the Equivalence Principle

Relativism, realism, and anti-realism all have their own disadvantages. Relativism is self-undermining and incorrectly treats some kinds of errors as impossible. Realism faces a challenge from skepticism. Anti-realism avoids skepticism by claiming everything true is knowable, but it comes at the cost of classical logic and faces a challenge from the Paradox of Knowability.

It is worth considering explicitly how each of these views fares with respect to the Equivalence Principle. In Chapter 1, we saw that the Equivalence Principle helped to explain how truth differs from belief. Unsurprisingly, it helps to explain the relativism's problems as well.

Given relativism, the Equivalence Schema itself is improperly formulated. The schema says 'It is true that _ if, and only if, _', but it does not specify true *for whom*. Subjectivists think truth is relative to individuals, and so there would have to be a version of the Equivalence Schema for each person, such as:

(17) It is true for Alice that _ if, and only if, _.
(18) It is true for Bob that _ if, and only if, _.
(19) It is true for Charlie that _ if, and only if, _.

and so on. If a claim's being true "for" someone is a matter of her believing it, though, the possibility of mistaken beliefs makes it easy to come up with counterexamples to these schemata. Suppose Alice thinks Abraham Lincoln was the first man on the moon. If (17) held, we would then have:

(20) It is true for Alice that Abraham Lincoln was the first man on the moon if, and only if, Abraham Lincoln was the first man on the moon.

Given that Alice thinks Abraham Lincoln was the first man on the moon, it would then follow that he *was* the first man on the moon! Subjectivism fails the Equivalence Principle's test. Consensus relativism fails for the same reason. It simply does not follow from the fact that anyone – any person, culture, class, race, gender, religion, or whatever – *believes* Abraham Lincoln was the first man on the moon that Abraham Lincoln *was* the first man on the moon. Nor does it follow from the claim that Abraham Lincoln was the first man on the moon that any individual or group happens to believe he was.

Anti-realism also faces a challenge from the Equivalence Principle. The hard cases for anti-realism come from T-biconditionals such as these:

(21) It is true that the last dinosaur died on a Wednesday if, and only if, the last dinosaur died on a Wednesday.

(22)   It is true that the last dinosaur did not die on a Wednesday if, and only if, the last dinosaur did not die on a
Wednesday.

Such T-biconditionals involve claims that are not just unknowable, but whose denials are unknowable too. (If you think
we can know whether or not the last dinosaur died on a
Wednesday, then feel free to substitute a different example,
such as one from the list earlier in this chapter.)

If, as anti-realism contends, truth is the same as knowability, then (21) and (22) mean the same as:

(23)   It is knowable that the last dinosaur died on a Wednesday if, and only if, the last dinosaur died on a
Wednesday.
(24)   It is knowable that the last dinosaur did not die on a
Wednesday if, and only if, the last dinosaur did not die
on a Wednesday.

Here is the problem. According to the classical logical law of
excluded middle, either the last dinosaur died on a Wednesday or the last dinosaur did not die on a Wednesday. For any
claim *c*, either *c* or its denial, not-*c*, is the case. Along with
(23) and (24), though, that implies that we can know whether
or not the last dinosaur died on a Wednesday after all. Thanks
to (23), we can know it if it did. Thanks to (24), we can know
it if it didn't. And thanks to the law of excluded middle, those
are the only possibilities: either it did or it didn't.

Anti-realism and classical logic are thus inconsistent with
the existence of unanswerable questions, but it seems indisputable that there are unanswerable questions. So, in order
to satisfy the Equivalence Principle, anti-realists have to reject
classical logic. They need to employ a non-classical logic that
lacks the law of excluded middle, can accommodate claims
that are neither true nor false, and that in particular can make
sense of biconditionals of the form 'It is true that _ if, and
only if, '_', when the '_'s are filled with sentences that are
neither true nor false.'

Realism, in contrast, faces none of these problems. Realists
think there is a mind-independent world, and the truth or

falsity of some claims depends on how things are in that world, irrespective of what anyone believes or what anyone could know. Suppose it is unknowable whether the last dinosaur died on a Wednesday, and no one has any opinion on the matter either. For realists, the truth or falsity of the claim that the last dinosaur died on a Wednesday depends on nothing other than the last dinosaur and when it died. If it is not true that the last dinosaur died on a Wednesday, then it did not die on a Wednesday. That is something anti-realists cannot guarantee.

Relativism is implausible. Anti-realism comes at the price of classical logic and positing surprising gaps in the world – not just in cases of vagueness, but in parts of mathematics, the distant past, the distant future, and faraway locations. Realism seems more promising than either of the alternatives discussed here.

But that is not to say that realism does not have its problems. To adopt a realist view of the nature of truth, one must take on obligations elsewhere in philosophy, especially in epistemology. One takes on the burden of answering the skeptical challenge, either by embracing the idea that we cannot know very much at all about the mind independent world, or by explaining how we could know how things really are, over and above how they seem to be. But this burden is bearable. Knowledge requires beliefs that are well enough supported, but it does not require them to be so well supported as to rule out all logical possibility of error. Of course, we must grant that is no easy take to say exactly how good is "good enough."

The realist's burdens are bearable. It is plausible that knowledge requires beliefs whose support is *good enough*, rather than support that rules out all logic possibilities of error. Though it is not entirely clear how good is "good enough," this much does seem to be clear. The skeptical demand that we rule out all logical possibility of error, including the possibility that we are deceived in ways it is in principle impossible for us to rule out, is unreasonable. The problem, non-skeptical realists can maintain, is that the skeptic sets the requirements for knowledge too high, not that we do not or cannot meet them.

Further Reading

René Descartes presents the thought experiment about the evil demon and grapples with the problem of skepticism in his *Meditations on First Philosophy* (Descartes 1641). David Hume outlines and defends his skeptical philosophy in the *Enquiry Concerning Human Understanding* (1777) and *Treatise of Human Nature* (1739). See especially Sections II–V of the *Enquiry*. Kant's great metaphysical work is the *Critique of Pure Reason* (1781), and the most important aspects of it are summarized in his *Prolegomena to Any Future Metaphysics* (1783). For more recent work on the skeptical problem, see the essays in Warfield & DeRose 1999.

Plato takes on Protagoras' relativism in the *Theaetetus*, and Aristotle argues against it in *Metaphysics* Book III (Γ). For a nice discussion of Aristotle's argument, see Evans 1974. See Salerno 2009 for some recent essays on the Paradox of Knowability.

The *Stanford Encyclopedia of Philosophy* contains several articles touching on the topics of this chapter and includes extensive lists of references. See in particular "Truth" (Glanzberg 2009), "Realism" (Miller 2012), "Relativism" (Swoyer 2010), "Skepticism" (Klein 2011), "Fitch's Paradox of Knowability" (Brogaard & Salerno 2012), and the articles on Hume and Kant.

3
Truth and Value

"The true," wrote William James, "is the name of whatever proves itself to be good in the way of belief, and good, too, for definite, assignable reasons" (1907a, p. 38). James's idea seems to have been that there is no separating truths nature from its value. 'True' names a particular sort of goodness for beliefs, and explaining what truth is means explaining what it is for beliefs to be good.

Some other philosophers, such as Michael Dummett (1958), have taken a similar view of the relationship between truth and statements that are correctly made. To understand what truth is, they think, is to understand a certain variety of rightness or correctness for statements. The nature of truth is that kind of correctness.

Even if these philosophers are wrong to think of truth as essentially a *kind* of goodness or rightness, truth does appear to be worth caring about. It is, in some sense, better to believe or assert what is true rather than what is false. Maybe truth is good for its own sake, or maybe it is only good for the sake of something else. Either way, a theory of the nature of truth should help us to make sense of truth's value. It should not leave us wondering why we should care whether our beliefs or statements are true.

This chapter addresses two questions about truth and value. First, is truth essentially a kind of goodness, as James and Dummett seem to think? Second, even if truth is not *essentially* a kind of goodness, why is truth worth caring about? What sort of value does truth have, if it has any at all?

3.1   Is Truth Essentially a Kind of Goodness?

A spherical tennis ball is a better tennis ball than a cubical one, but that is not part of the essence of being a sphere. It is better for stop signs to be red than green, but that is not part of the nature of redness. Unlike shape and color properties, some properties seem to have matters of value or obligation built into them. It is part of the nature of murder that a murder is a *morally wrong* killing; being morally wrong is part of what makes a killing a murder. It might be part of the nature of justice that just policies treat people rightly; treating people rightly is part of the nature of justice. Beauty too seems to have this feature. Beauty isn't just aesthetically desirable, it is a kind of aesthetic goodness. Philosophers call properties like these "normative."

It is, in some sense, better for beliefs or statements to be true than to be false. But is that part of the nature of truth itself? Is truth a normative property, like justice, beauty, or being a murder, or is it a property like redness or roundness instead?

Those who think truth is a normative property often seem to reason in the following way:

(1) If it is part of the concept of truth that true beliefs or statements are better than false ones, then truth is a normative property.
(2) It is part of the concept of truth that true beliefs or statements are better than false ones.
(3) Therefore, truth is essentially a kind of goodness.

Although there may be some room to doubt the first premise of this argument, philosophers have tended to focus their attention on (2).

It is important to take note of some things that (2) does not say. It does not say that it is better for any *claim* to be true than untrue. For example, the following claim is true, but its truth is not a good thing:

(4)   Approximately 1 billion people currently live in conditions of absolute poverty.

Premise (2) is about beliefs and statements, not the claims they express. Nor does it say true beliefs and statements are always better than false ones all things considered. Some true beliefs are so dangerous we would be better off without them, and some true statements are so hurtful we shouldn't make them. In (2) what matters is the idea that beliefs are better, *taken simply as beliefs*, when they are true than when they are false, and that statements are better, *taken simply as statements*, when they are true, although any particular true belief or statement might be objectionable on other grounds, all things considered.

William James was struck by the fact that deciding whether something is true is no different from deciding whether to believe it. The point of the concept of truth, he thought, was to label those beliefs that hold up under testing and prove themselves useful. On such a view, the concept of truth includes the idea that true beliefs are better than false ones because 'truth' is just the name for the good in the way of belief. As discussed in detail in the next chapter, James's view suffers serious problems, not least that beliefs can be good in the way he has in mind without being true.

Michael Dummett (1958) is another influential source of the idea that truth is essentially a kind of goodness. In a famous passage, he writes:

> Let us compare truth and falsity with the winning and losing of a board game. For a particular game we may imagine first formulating the rules by specifying the initial position and the permissible moves; the game comes to an end when there is no permissible move. We may then distinguish between two (or three) kinds of final position, which we call "Win" (meaning that the player to make the first move wins), "Lose" (similarly) and possibly "Draw." Unless we tacitly appeal to the usual meanings of the words "win," "lose" and "draw," this description leaves out one vital point – that it is the object

of a player to win. It is part of the concept of winning a game
that a player plays to win, and this part of the concept is not
conveyed by a classification of the end positions into winning
ones and losing ones. We can imagine a variant of chess in
which it is the object of each player to be checkmated, and
this would be an entirely different game; but the formal
description we imagined would coincide with the formal
description of chess. The whole theory of chess could be formulated with reference only to the formal description; but
which theorems of this theory interested us would depend
upon whether we wished to play chess or the variant game.
Likewise, it is part of the concept of truth that we aim at
making true statements ... (p. 143)

To say "we aim at making true statements" is to say something about what sort of statements it is good to make, or
what sort of statements one ought to make. When you make
a statement, you ought to make sure what you say is true.
Otherwise, you are doing it wrong in some way. If you are
trying to be deceptive, what you are doing is like cheating in
the game of making statements. If you are simply uncon-
cerned with whether what you have said is true or false, your
statements are like the moves of a player who is pushing the
pieces around without trying to win, hardly playing the game
at all.

Suppose Alice knows perfectly well what board positions
are called "winning" and "losing" in every game, but she
does not know that, in games, the players are trying to win.
Alice has mastered the descriptive part of the difference
between winning and losing, but she still does not understand
the concept of winning. She has not grasped the normative
difference between winning and losing. "Winning" is the
good member of the pair, the state one aims to achieve.
"Losing" is the bad one, the state one aims to avoid. Dummett
thinks the case is similar with truth and falsehood. Bob might
know perfectly well what it takes for any given statement to
qualify as true. If he does not know that we aim to make true
rather than false statements, though, he has failed to grasp
the normative difference between truth and falsehood. He
does not understand that it is good for statements to be true,
in a way entirely different from the way it is good for them
to be audible, bad for them to be indecipherable, and neutral

for them to be made in the morning. To understand truth *as truth*, on Dummett's view, one must understand it as our goal in making statements.

Even if Dummett is right about winning, though, there is plenty of room to deny his claims about truth. One could well maintain that Bob understands the concept of truth perfectly well, but he has failed to properly understand what it means to make a statement. It could be part of the concept of *assertion* or of a *statement* that we aim at stating what is true, but not part of the concept of truth at all.

Consider another analogy with games. In chess, the goal is to achieve a board position in which one's opponent's king is in checkmate. In suicide chess, the goal is to achieve a board position in which one's *own* king is in checkmate, but the other rules of the game are exactly the same as in ordinary chess. Suppose Carol knows perfectly well how to tell if a king is in checkmate, but she does not know how checkmate figures into the goals of chess and suicide chess. The problem is not that Carol lacks the concept of checkmate; it is that she does not yet understand what *chess* and *suicide chess* are. Those are the concepts she has not mastered. One could understand Bob's situation as analogous to Carol's. Bob knows what it takes for a statement to be true or to be false, but he does not grasp that truth is our aim when we make statements. This could be because he has not fully grasped what *statements* are, although he understands the concepts of truth and falsity just fine.

Checkmate and truth may be normatively important properties. One is our aim in playing chess, the other our aim in making statements. But they do not have to be normative properties in order to be normatively important in those ways. The difference between chess and suicide chess lies in whether they take checkmate to be a way of winning or losing. The difference between making sincere assertions and blowing hot air lies in whether one is aiming to say only what is true.

Some writers seem to suggest a different line of argument for the conclusion that truth is essentially a kind of goodness (Engel 2005; Wright 1992; Lynch 2005b; 2009a). When a statement is true, we call it "right" or "correct," and we call false statements "wrong" or "incorrect." The terms 'right' and 'true', when applied to statements, seem to be synonyms, and so one might argue in this way:

(5) As applied to statements, 'true' and 'right' are synonyms.
(6) If two terms are synonyms, they express the same concept.
(7) 'Right' expresses the concept of rightness, which is normative.
(8) So, 'true', as applied to statements, expresses the concept of rightness, which is normative.

Does this argument work?

There is no denying that we sometimes use such terms as 'right', 'wrong', 'correct', 'incorrect', 'error', and 'mistake' in connection with truth and falsehood. When what you say is true, it is "right," and what you say is "wrong" when it is false.

None of that suffices to show 'true' and 'right' express the same concept, though. You might describe a place setting as having the dinner fork to the left of the plate, or you might note that the fork is in the right place. Even though the fork is in the right place if and only if it is to the left of the plate, 'to the left of the plate' and 'in the right place' clearly do not express the same concept. The former just describes where the fork is. The latter applies a set of rules and evaluates the fork's position as conforming to those rules or not.

Even if statements are "right" if and only if they are true, 'right' and 'true' need not be synonyms. To call a statement true could be a matter of merely describing it, while calling it right is a matter of evaluating it positively in relation to a set of rules. The argument's first premise, then, is not obviously correct.

Even given that premise, though, there is room to doubt (7), the claim that 'right' (in a sense plausibly synonymous with 'true') expresses a normative concept. When we call *actions* right or wrong, we are evaluating them in light of some set of rules or standards (often, moral standards). Perhaps, though, 'right' expresses a different concept when applied to statements from what it expresses when applied to actions or place settings, just as it does in such expressions as 'right angle'. You say there are seven days in a week, and I say, "That's right." In saying that, it is plausible that I am simply expressing my agreement with you about how many days there are in a week, not making a normative evaluation of your statements as good or bad, permissible or impermissible, or something else.

None of this proves that truth is *not* a normative property, but it does cast doubt on some of the main reasons philosophers have given for thinking it is. Even if truth is not a normative property, though, we still tend to think it is worth caring about. Let us consider, then, what might make truth worth caring about. What sort of value does truth have?

3.2 What Makes Truth Valuable?

Though philosophers have discussed a dizzying variety of kinds of value, five kinds are especially important in considering the value of truth. Each represents a way in which philosophers have claimed truth is valuable or worth caring about:

- *Intrinsic value.* It is good in itself for beliefs to be true.
- *Final value.* Truth is valuable insofar as rational beings care about it.
- *Instrumental value.* Truth is valuable because it makes beliefs more useful.
- *Constitutive value.* Truth is worth caring about because caring about truth is a necessary part of living a good life.
- *Telic value.* Truth is worth caring about because we benefit from caring about it.

Let us examine these one by one.

3.2.1 Is Truth Intrinsically Valuable?

Some people think truth is valuable "for its own sake." One thing that might mean is that truth is *intrinsically* valuable.

When something is intrinsically valuable, it is valuable in itself, by its own nature, and not because of its relationship to anything else. Treating people kindly might be good in and of itself, regardless of whether it also makes people likely to return the favor and be nice to you. On the other hand, the value of an ordinary hammer derives not from what it is but from what one can do with it. An ordinary hammer probably isn't intrinsically valuable, but kindness might be.

The idea that truth is intrinsically valuable is a version of the idea that truth is good "for its own sake." It is the idea that, other things being equal, true beliefs are better than false ones, and they are better simply by virtue of being true. They have value that comes from the nature of truth itself and not just from the relationship of true belief to other valuable things.

One way to argue for the conclusion that something is intrinsically valuable is to argue that, as a matter of fact, we tend to care about it for its own sake. Caring about something for its own sake usually involves thinking of it as intrinsically valuable. So, unless we are much mistaken in our values, the things we care about for their own sakes will tend to be intrinsically valuable. One thus might argue for the intrinsic value of truth in particular on the grounds that we do tend to desire it for its own sake, or we tend to prefer true beliefs to false ones, simply because they are true. Do we?

Michael Lynch (2005b, pp. 15–19) has proposed the following thought experiment (based on Nozick [1977]) intended to show that most people do care about truth for its own sake. Imagine you have the choice between two ways the rest of your life could work out. If you choose Option A, nothing will change. If you choose Option B, you will live out your days hooked into a computer like the one in *The Matrix*. Your subjective experiences will be just as if you had chosen Option A, and you will forget you ever made the choice. So far as you are concerned, you will be living in the real world, interacting with real people, eating real food, etc., but it will be an illusion. Although it will make no difference to how things seem to you or to how happy you are, almost all your beliefs about the outside world will be false. Most people, Lynch thinks, would prefer Option A to Option B, and he thinks this means they care about truth for its own sake; they think of truth as intrinsically valuable.

Lynch's thought experiment does not prove much. The trouble is that there are reasons to prefer Option A to Option B that have nothing to do with truth's value. For example, suppose Bob loves his dying mother, and he wants to comfort her in her last days. Bob does not want to *merely seem* to comfort his mother, he wants to really comfort her. He does not want his mother to die alone while he has experiences exactly as if he were comforting her. Even if Bob is utterly indifferent to truth, he has reason to prefer Option A because, in Option A, he gets what he wants instead of only seeming to get what he wants.

True beliefs aren't the only things you lose if you choose Option B. You also trade the actual accomplishment of your goals for the illusion of accomplishing them. Consequently, we cannot conclude that people tend to value truth for its own sake, simply because they prefer Option A to Option B.

Jonathan Kvanvig (2008) has suggested a different thought experiment meant to show we tend to think of truth as good for its own sake. He asks us to imagine two beings who are completely equal with respect to the fulfillment of their needs and the accomplishment of their goals. One of them is omniscient (that is, believes everything true and nothing false), while the other is not. The omniscient being seems better off than the non-omniscient being. Since the two beings are equally well off with respect to fulfilling their needs and accomplishing their goals, it would appear that the omniscient being is better off just because it has more true beliefs. If we think the omniscient being's true beliefs make it better off, just by being true, that indicates we think of truth as good for its own sake.

This way of arguing for the intrinsic value of truth has two main disadvantages. First, all it can hope to show is that truth has *some* intrinsic value; it cannot tell us how valuable truth is. Second, the best explanation for why the omniscient being seems to be better off might have nothing to do with the value of truth.

The first disadvantage might appear minor at first, but consider a variation on Kvanvig's thought experiment. In the variation, the non-omniscient being does slightly *better* than the omniscient one at fulfilling its needs and accomplishing its goals. The omniscient being has more true beliefs, but the other being now seems better off overall, even if only slightly. While the omniscient being seems better off when the two are *equal* in all other respects, if the non-omniscient being does *better* to any extent, in any other respect, it is no longer so obvious that the omniscient being really is better off at all. Even if the omniscient being's extra true beliefs have some value, that value appears to be very easily outweighed by any other good at all.

Given how easy it is to outweigh truth's intrinsic value, one might suspect that value is an illusion in the first place. Perhaps there is an alternative explanation for why the omniscient being strikes us as better off in the original thought experiment. As it happens, there are at least two plausible alternatives.

The first starts from the idea that truth is the goal of beliefs. That is, part of what it means to have beliefs is to prefer believing what is true to believing what is false. If that idea is correct, our response to the original thought experiment is unsurprising. The omniscient being is doing better *as a believer*, but that is because of the nature of belief, not the nature of truth. True belief, on this view, is like fast running. A faster runner is better, as a runner, than a slower one. That, however, is because running, by nature, aims for speed, not because speed, by nature, is the aim of running.

It is a matter of some controversy whether belief aims for truth in this way. A second alternative explanation depends instead on two important psychological facts. First, people tend to attribute their successes to internal causes, such as their competency or the truth of their beliefs, rather than to external circumstances (de Jong et al. 1988), but they offer the opposite explanations of their failures. Second, when we associate one thing with something else we value, we come to value the first thing for its own sake as well (De Houwer et al. 2001). In light of the first fact, we should expect people to associate true believing with successful action. In light of the second fact, we should expect that association to make people value truth for its own sake. It is only to be expected, then, that we would value truth for its own sake, and we would think of the omniscient being as better off – even if truth had no intrinsic value whatsoever. Since we would have those attitudes whether or not truth is intrinsically valuable, we should not put too much confidence in the intuitions that drive Kvanvig's thought experiment.

Of course, that does not prove truth *isn't* intrinsically valuable, but it does suggest we lack a compelling reason for thinking it is. The psychological explanation given above casts doubt on any argument for truth's intrinsic value that turns on our tendency, as a matter of fact, to care about truth for its own sake. If that explanation is correct, proponents of truth's intrinsic value will have to support their position on different grounds.

Intrinsic value is not the only kind of value, and it is not the only thing that could make truth worth caring about. Philosophers have also claimed truth has some other, extrinsic, type of value. One of them, "final value," gives a different sense in which truth might be good "for its own sake."

3.2.2 Does Truth Have Final Value?

The idea of final value comes from Christine Korsgaard (1983), who argues that something can be good for its own sake without being intrinsically valuable. Korsgaard is part of a Kantian philosophical tradition, according to which it is deeply morally significant that rational beings have goals and desire some things for their own sake. To desire something for its own sake, recall, is to desire it for what it is, and not just for such reasons as that it might be useful or helpful in getting something else.

A stamp collector, for example, might want to amass a diverse collection of stamps, but not for the sake of selling it or for any other purpose. Instead, she simply wants it, just for itself. One of her life goals is to amass such a collection. The value of a diverse collection of stamps is not intrinsic to it, but there does seems to be something good about the stamp collector achieving her goal of a diverse collection. Furthermore, if a vandal destroys the collection, it seems as though the vandal has done a harm to the collector by destroying something of value, and that would be the case even if no one else in the world cared about stamps at all.

The collection seems to get value simply from the fact that the collector values it for its own sake. 'Final value' is Korsgaard's phrase for the kind of value things have by virtue of being desired for their own sake.

We can make a case that truth has final value in two ways. First, we might note that, as a matter of fact, people do care about or desire truth for its own sake. That attitude is reflected in our reactions to thought experiments such as Kvanvig's. It is also reflected in an attitude expressed by Lynch (2009a) and Kvanvig (2008), that the only reason we don't care to learn certain trivial truths (such as the truth about how many blades of grass are in the yard) is that we have more pressing needs to attend to.

A second case for truth's final value makes a bolder claim. Not only *do* we care about truth for its own sake, but we *must*. One cannot have beliefs without taking them to represent the world accurately and managing them in ways designed to keep them answerable to the external world. To have beliefs, one must enforce a "mind to world direction of fit" on them, ditching false beliefs just because they are false, and keeping or forming true beliefs just because they are true. To be a rational creature is, in part, to have beliefs, and so it is inevitable that rational creatures would value truth for its own sake. It would then be equally inevitable that truth has final value.

The second argument turns on the idea that nothing can have beliefs without caring about truth for its own sake. A potential problem is that only a creature with the concept of truth can value truth for its own sake. So, on this view, only a creature with the concept of truth (and the ability to value it) could possibly have beliefs at all. Some philosophers are happy to make the concept of truth a prerequisite for having beliefs, but it has quite counter-intuitive consequences. It implies that non-human animals (and many small children) don't have beliefs. For example, it would mean that a dog cannot believe the squirrel it is chasing has run up a tree, and the squirrel has no beliefs about where it has buried its acorns. Rather than deny that dogs, squirrels, and toddlers have any beliefs, the more plausible route would be to deny that having beliefs requires caring about truth for its own sake.

Once we have set aside the second argument, we can more easily see what is wrong with the first line of argument as well. Although we generally do care about truth for its own sake, that is hardly a way in which it is good. People can value anything for its own sake, from justice to rare stamps to the pain of others. Despite Korsgaard's claims, things do not become valuable just because people value them. Stamp collections and torture do not acquire a special kind of value from the fact that people value them for their own sakes. So-called "final value" is not a real kind of value at all. If anything, it is a way of being *valued*, not a way of being *valuable*.

The idea of final value involves a subtle confusion. There is something good – maybe even intrinsically good – about people getting what they want. That could be so even if what a person wants is as boring as a stamp or as repugnant as torturing babies. To acknowledge that, though, we do not have to suppose the actual objects of people's desires have a special kind of value, but only that there is something good about the satisfaction of people's desires, apart from the value of what is desired.

There is little reason to suppose truth is good "for its own sake," either by being intrinsically valuable or by being finally valuable. Truth might still be valuable in some other way, though. Almost all philosophers interested in the value of truth think it as least *instrumentally* valuable – which is to say that it makes beliefs useful or helpful in getting us what we want. Let us consider that idea next.

3.2.3   Is Truth Instrumentally Valuable?

A hammer is useful for driving nails. It is instrumentally valuable for building things. Money is instrumentally valuable. It derives value from the value of what we can buy with it. Philosophers tend to think truth is instrumentally valuable as well. Not only can true beliefs come in handy for doing such things as getting food and treating diseases, but false beliefs can have disastrous consequences. People who shoot themselves accidentally, for example, are often injured because they falsely believe a gun isn't loaded. Since true beliefs can be so useful, and false ones so dangerous, it is understandable that one might think of truth itself as instrumentally valuable.

The question of truth's instrumental value, though, is considerably more complicated than this. Sometimes, our true beliefs hurt us. If your plane is going to crash in the mountains, it could be fatal to believe the truth about when it is going to take off (Stich 1990). Some false beliefs are very useful and helpful, especially those that psychologists call "positive illusions" (Taylor 1989). Furthermore, we typically act on a mixture of true beliefs and false ones. The helpfulness of any particular belief, true or false, depends on what else you believe and the external circumstances in which you act. It can be difficult, or impossible, to factor out the contribution of a particular belief's truth or falsity to the success or failure of a particular action.

A plausible alternative is to see truth as a symptom or a rough approximation of the sort of complex fit between belief, behavior, and environment that makes for successful action. Then it would be a mistake to say that truth is instrumentally valuable. Even if true beliefs often help us to succeed in our actions, that does not mean their truth *makes* them useful. By analogy, suppose all the sturdy hammers have been painted blue, while the flimsy ones have been painted yellow. The blue hammers are thus better for driving nails, but their blueness does not help them drive the nails. Likewise, true beliefs might tend to be more helpful to us than false ones, but it does not follow that their truth *makes* them more helpful. Like the blueness of the hammers, it could instead be a feature that happens to be correlated with another feature that does all the work. Strictly speaking, the property of truth would not be instrumentally valuable in that case.

Even if truth is not instrumentally valuable in the strict sense of actually playing a role in getting us what we want, we do seems to be in a better position to get what we want when our beliefs are more rather than less accurate. That does seem to be something good about having true beliefs. The hard part is to find the right way to characterize that sort of goodness.

Recently, some philosophers interested in the value of truth have shifted their focus from the value of truth itself to the value of *caring about truth*. One of those philosophers is Michael Lynch, who argues that truth is worth caring about because caring about truth is part of living a good human life (2005b).

3.2.4 Is Caring about Truth a Constitutive Good?

As Lynch uses the term, a "constitutive good" is something that is an essential part of a good and flourishing life (pp. 128–9). For example, a loving attitude might not only be instrumentally valuable (because it makes people like you), but having such an attitude might be an essential part of what it means to live well as a human. A loving attitude would then count, in Lynch's terminology, as a constitutive good.

Lynch thinks the attitude of caring about truth for its own sake or, more briefly, "caring about truth," is a constitutive good, and he thinks that makes truth worth caring about. He thinks truth is worth caring about because one must care about truth to live a good human life.

On Lynch's view, caring about truth means

> manifest[ing] particular character traits that are oriented toward the truth. It involves being willing to hear both sides of the story, being open-minded and tolerant of others' opinions, being careful and sensitive to detail, and paying close attention to the evidence. And it also involves being willing to question assumptions, giving and asking for reasons, being impartial, and being intellectually courageous. (Lynch 2005b, pp. 129–30)

In addition to the kinds of traits Lynch mentions, we might add another element: willingness to assess the reliability of one's methods of forming opinions, and to make adjustments to those methods aimed at increasing their reliability (Wrenn 2005).

Lynch argues as follows (2005b, p. 136):

(1) If intellectual integrity is an essential part of living a good life, then so is caring about truth as such.

(2)   Intellectual integrity is an essential part of living a good life.

(3)   Therefore, caring about truth as such is an essential part of living a good life.

(4)   If caring about truth is an essential part of living a good life, then truth as such is worth caring about for its own sake.

(5)   Therefore, truth is worth caring about for its own sake.

By 'intellectual integrity', Lynch means willingness to "stand up for your best judgment of the truth, by being willing to act in accordance with that judgment when the need arises" (p. 131). He thinks it is impossible to have intellectual integrity without caring about truth. So, he thinks, caring about truth is an essential part of intellectual integrity and thus of living a good life.

Lynch also gives a second reason to think caring about truth is part of living a good life. Living well, he thinks, requires happiness. Happiness requires self-respect, and self-respect requires that one be willing to make sacrifices for what one thinks is right. Such willingness, Lynch claims, requires the dispositions that constitute caring about truth (p. 135).

Lynch's account suffers two serious problems. First, it depends on an incorrect notion of intellectual integrity. Second, it is doubtful that self-respect requires the sort of concern for truth Lynch says it does.

To have intellectual integrity, according to Lynch, is to be willing to "stand up" for the truth, which means being willing to act in accordance with your judgment of what is true when the need arises. Your judgment of what is true, though, is just whatever you happen to believe. If you believe something is true, that just means you believe it. So, what Lynch calls "intellectual integrity" amounts to being willing to act in accordance with what you believe, when the need arises. However, *whenever* a person acts, she acts in accordance with what she believes. Even if I am forced at gunpoint to act as though $2 + 3 = 6$ (something I don't believe), I act in accordance with my belief that *someone will kill me if I don't pretend $2 + 3 = 6$*. So, having what Lynch calls "intellectual integrity" is just a matter of being willing to act when necessary. That might be a virtue, but it isn't intellectual integrity. Rather, it is something in the neighborhood of courage, conscientiousness, or diligence.

The first premise of Lynch's argument is thus dubious. Why should courage, conscientiousness, or diligence require one to care about truth? Why do I have to pay close attention to the evidence and be tolerant of others' opinions in order to be willing to act when action is necessary?

Lynch also thinks you must care about truth for its own sake in order to have self-respect. His idea is that you cannot be willing to make sacrifices for what you believe is right unless you have the dispositions that constitute concern for truth. This too seems to be a mistake. Imagine a fanatical adherent of a totalitarian ideology, who is closed minded and intolerant, and who believes it is right to suppress and censor views contrary to the Party. Such a person might be quite willing to make great sacrifices for the sake of what she thinks is right. In her case, standing up for what she thinks is right would mean exhibiting precisely the *opposite* of the dispositions Lynch identifies with caring about truth.

If a good life requires caring about truth for its own sake, it isn't because that attitude is necessary for self-respect or in order to stand up for what one thinks is right. Someone can respect herself quite well without being a careful thinker, or stand up for what she thinks is right without paying any attention to evidence.

Lynch's argument does not show that truth is something we should care about, but a similar approach can be made to work. Instead of concentrating on constitutive value and the idea that caring about truth is an essential *part* of a good life, we can focus on a different sort of value, which I call "telic" value. Things have telic value when it is beneficial or advantageous to care about them.

3.2.5   Is Truth Telically Valuable?

Some things, like a delicious meal or a kind disposition, are good to have, and some things are good to *strive for*. Imagine a mountain climber. To climb a mountain is to try to reach the top, and there may be some value in standing on top of

in. To a climber, though, there is satisfaction and
ı trying to reach the top, over and above whatever
e is in actually reaching it.

ıg the top of a mountain has two kinds of value for
a climber. First, it has something like instrumental value,
because it is a cause of good feelings in the climber. Second,
though, it has telic value. By making it her goal to reach the
summit, the climber benefits in other ways. She gains the
satisfaction of making the climb, which differs from the satisfaction of reaching the top and from the satisfaction of
randomly wandering around on the mountainside.

With the concept of telic value, we can set aside or be
neutral on questions about the value of true beliefs themselves, and we can focus instead on how we benefit from
caring about truth. Caring about truth means having various
dispositions, such as open-mindedness, concern for the reliability of one's methods of inquiry, etc. Even if such dispositions are not necessary for living a good life, they might
benefit us. If they do, truth has telic value. So, do we benefit
from having those dispositions?

A preliminary yes answer comes from a study conducted
by the psychologist Nansook Park and her colleagues, Christopher Peterson and Martin Seligman (Park, Peterson, &
Seligman 2004). They found that people who rate more
highly on measures of curiosity, open-mindedness, critical
thinking, and love of learning also report higher levels of
satisfaction with their lives. If those traits constitute caring
about truth, then it would appear that people who care more
about truth also lead more satisfying lives.

The psychologists' findings are not the last word on the
matter though. Their results are consistent with many alternative possibilities. Perhaps having a good life causes one to
become more curious and open-minded, to love learning
more, and to think more critically. Or maybe caring about
truth makes you more willing to accept your life as it is,
increasing your satisfaction without making you better off.
We cannot rule out such alternative possibilities without
much more work.

Despite the ambiguity of the psychologists' results, we can
identify some benefits we stand to gain from caring about

truth. Even if truth is not instrumentally valuable in a strict sense, it does seem that we are better poised to accomplish our goals, the more accurate our relevant beliefs. That is a reason to care about truth, just as the tendency of sturdy hammers to be blue can give one a reason to care about the color of the hammer one is about to use. Caring about truth can help us to get into position to accomplish our goals, by helping us to get and maintain an accurate view of how things are.

Caring about truth could also make it easier for us to enjoy certain collective goods. A collective good is a good whose achievement requires teamwork. It takes three other people to make a four-part harmony, and so a four-part harmony is a collective good. Some other collective goods might include language, basketball games, and readily available, reliable health care.

To enjoy collective goods, we have to coordinate our activities, often with great complexity. If I care about truth, and so do you, then we have a very useful tool for anticipating one another's actions and coordinating ourselves. Imagine trying to make plans with someone who *doesn't* particularly care about the truth of his beliefs. You might agree to meet at Chuck's Café, but your friend might be wrong about where Chuck's is. For your friend to get to the right place, he needs to care enough about truth to correct his false belief. Otherwise, you will be waiting at Chuck's, and he might be sitting in the lobby of the Department of Motor Vehicles, wondering where you are and ignoring all the evidence that he is in the wrong place.

If you and I both care about truth, we will tend to believe pretty much the same things in the same circumstances. When we disagree, we will be in a position to resolve our disagreement rationally, by open-mindedly considering the evidence and its significance. This makes the coordination of our behavior easier. You can anticipate my behavior because you can anticipate my beliefs, and you can anticipate my beliefs because they will be pretty much the same as yours.

The dispositions involved in caring about truth are dispositions that root out error and help to ensure one's beliefs are accurate. Such dispositions are not only useful in the pursuit of one's individual goals. They also help us to anticipate one another's behavior and coordinate ourselves in pursuit of collective goods.

3.3 Conclusion

We care about truth. We want people to tell us the honest truth, and we all try, at least to some extent, to make sure we believe what is true rather than false. Caring about truth gives us a reason to want a good answer to the question, "What is truth?" A good answer to that question must, at the very least, be compatible with whatever sort of value truth has, and it might need to go further, making it clear how truth is a kind of goodness for beliefs or statements.

This chapter has surveyed several ways of understanding the value of truth. One is that truth itself is a normative property – for a belief or statement to be true is for it to be good in a particular way. Although arguments such as Dummett's fail to show truth is a normative property, the idea has been influential in recent work on the nature of truth, as will be seen in later chapters.

Regardless of whether truth is normative, it still might be intrinsically, finally, instrumentally, or telically valuable, or the attitude of caring about truth might be part of the good human life. This chapter has reviewed some reasons philosophers have thought of the value of truth in each of these ways. In most cases, the arguments have been weak, but there is good reason to think truth is at least telically valuable.

Further Reading

One of the best and most accessible recent discussions of the value of truth is Michael Lynch's book, *True to Life* (Lynch 2005b).

Dummett's discussion of the analogy of truth to winning is his (1958), and the idea that truth is essentially a kind of success figures in the last chapter of Searle (1995). Crispin Wright (1992) draws on Dummett's idea in developing a type of pluralist theory of truth (see Chapter 7 of this book) and approaching debates about realism and anti-realism. Pascal Engel (2002) also draws on Dummett's insights, with results quite different from Wright's.

For discussions of the intrinsic value of truth, see Lynch (2009a) and Kvanvig (2008). Wrenn (2010) criticizes the view that truth is instrumentally valuable. McGrath (2005) includes additional objections to Lynch's idea that caring about truth has constitutive value.

4
Epistemic Theories of Truth

We can now begin surveying some answers to the question, 'What is truth?'. We will evaluate each answer by considering each of the following:

- How plausible is the theory itself? Are there strong arguments in its favor?
- Does the theory preserve the non-paradoxical instances of the Equivalence Schema?
- Is the theory compatible with realism, and is it compatible with anti-realism?
- Does the theory help to make sense of the value of truth?

This chapter concerns so-called *epistemic* theories of truth. The word 'epistemic' comes from a Greek word for knowledge, and these theories explain the nature of truth by appeal to the notions of knowledge or, more commonly, justified belief.

4.1 Skepticism and What Our Tests Test

There is a single core insight behind epistemic theories of truth. We'll call it the Test Principle, and it says:

> *Test Principle*: Whatever truth is, it is what our tests for truth test for, and so it is a property claims have if they pass those tests and lack if they fail them.

"Our tests for truth" are a varied lot. They include all our ways of finding out about the world, from looking in the refrigerator to find out whether any milk is left, to doing mathematical proofs, to the immensely complex apparatus of modern science. But they all serve a common purpose. We use them all to find true answers to the questions we care about.

It is hard to see how knowledge could be possible if the Test Principle were false. Our only way to acquire knowledge is to apply our methods of inquiry. If those methods did not amount to tests for truth, we would have no particular reason to accept as true the claims our methods of inquiry recommend. If a true claim passed our tests, and we accepted it, we would be lucky, but we would not *know* the claim is true. Knowledge requires more than good luck. Skepticism, though, is not a plausible position. We know all manner things, and we know them on the basis of our methods of inquiry. So, it seems, the Test Principle or something very much like it must be correct.

Given the Test Principle, we can reasonably ask, what do our tests for truth test for? What property do the claims that pass our tests have in common that distinguishes them from claims that fail? If we can identify that property, epistemicists think, we will be able to understand the nature of truth. Moreover, they think, there is a straightforward answer to the question of what that property is: it is the property of *passing our tests for truth*.

The two most important epistemic theories of truth are the *coherence theory* and the *pragmatic theory*. They differ in the details of how they understand our tests for truth and what it means to pass them, but they share the idea that passing our tests for truth is all there is to being true.

To understand how these theories work, it might be helpful to consider an analogy with another case. According to one theory of what colors are, *redness* is just the property of looking red to normal observers in normal viewing conditions. To test something for redness, we look at it in normal conditions and see whether it looks red or not. On this view of colors, then there is no difference between being red and passing that test. Epistemicists think of truth in a similar way. We have various ways of testing claims for truth, and there is no difference between passing those tests and being true.

4.2 The Coherence Theory of Truth

A historically important epistemic theory of truth is the *coherence* theory. It can be stated as follows:

> *Coherence Theory of Truth*: For a claim to be true is for it to be part of a suitably coherent and comprehensive set of beliefs.

Before we can evaluate this theory, we need to get clear on what is meant by *coherence* and *comprehensiveness*.

Traditionally, philosophers have thought of coherence as requiring, at a minimum, logical consistency. A coherent set of beliefs should not contradict itself. A set of beliefs that includes both 'The earth is millions of years old' and 'The earth is not millions of years old' is inconsistent and, for that reason, not coherent. But mere consistency is not enough for the sort of coherence that is supposed to engender truth. The beliefs must also hang together in the right sort of way. Usually, this "right sort of way" involves explanatory connections among the beliefs. For example, the following set of beliefs is consistent, but it lacks the sort of connections coherentists think of truth as requiring:

(1) All poodles are hairless.
(2) $1 + 1 = 12$
(3) Electrons have positive charge.

To be coherent, each member of a set of beliefs must be explained by, and play a role in explaining, other members of the set.

Some philosophers think a coherence theory of truth is particularly apt for ethics (e.g., Quine 1981). Our moral beliefs include moral principles, concerning what features make things morally good or bad, as well as particular judgments about the moral value of certain actions or states of affairs. We can explain or justify our particular judgments by drawing on the general principles, and we can explain or justify the general principles by showing how they hang together as a coherent moral theory and fit with our particular judgments about cases. Some philosophers think that is all there is to say about moral truth. They think, ultimately, that what makes a moral belief true is nothing but the way it hangs together with other beliefs, and all that makes a moral belief false is the way it fails to hang together with other beliefs.

Coherentists also tend to require the set of beliefs in question to be *comprehensive* in scope. It must constitute a system that covers all topics. If any claim is capable of being true or false, either it or its negation must be part of the system. This requirement ensures that any suitably coherent system of beliefs will determine truth values for all claims capable of having them.

Why should anyone think of truth as coherence? Brand Blanshard (1939) articulated a main reason. His argument runs like this:

(4) Our only test of the truth of a claim is to see how well it fits or coheres with the rest of what we (ideally) believe; we accept as true claims that do cohere with our beliefs (including those we gain through observation), and we reject as false claims that contradict our other beliefs.

(5) To be true is to pass our test for truth, and to be false is to fail it.

(6) Therefore, to be true is to cohere with the rest of what we (ideally) believe.

The first premise refers to what we "ideally" believe. This is because no one's *actual* beliefs are either consistent or comprehensive. There is thus ample room for claims to cohere with someone's actual beliefs without being true. All the same, on Blanshard's view, the only way we can test any claim for truth is to see how well it fits with what we believe, and over time we adjust our body of beliefs to approximate the ideal of overall coherence and comprehensiveness more and more closely. The idea of truth is the idea of being a part of the ideal system of belief we are aiming for.

4.3 Problems for Coherentism

One of the most important objections to coherentism is the *alternative coherent systems* problem. It arises so long as we suppose there is more than one way the world might have been. Even if there is milk in the refrigerator, for example, that is by no means metaphysically necessary. The world could have been different in various ways that would involve there being no milk in the refrigerator – or even there being no refrigerators at all.

Imagine two complete descriptions of the world, which I will call MILKY and DRY. MILKY is a complete description of how the world would be in all respects if there were milk in the refrigerator. DRY is a complete description of how the world would be in all respects if there were no milk in the refrigerator. Both MILKY and DRY are possible comprehensive, coherent systems of beliefs.

Here is the problem for coherentism. The following claim:

(7)   There is milk in the refrigerator.

Fits with MILKY. Since MILKY is a suitably comprehensive and coherent set of beliefs, it then follows from coherentism that (7) is true. However, (7) also *fails* to fit with DRY, and DRY is also a suitably comprehensive and coherent set of beliefs. So, given coherentism, (7) then has to be false as well. We are thus left with the absurd situation that 'There is milk in the refrigerator' is both true and false. (Likewise, it comes out that 'There is no milk in the refrigerator' is both true and false, since it fits with DRY but not with MILKY.)

We can generalize this problem. For almost any non-contradictory claim, there is a possible coherent and comprehensive set of beliefs including that claim, as well as one that includes its denial. Consequently, coherentism seems to imply that almost everything is true and almost everything is false. Clearly, something is wrong.

To avoid this problem, coherentists need to identify some one, special set of beliefs, such that coherence with *that* set, and no other, constitutes truth. But what set is that? The two most popular options are *the beliefs one actually has* and *the ideal set of beliefs*.

The beliefs one actually has cannot serve the purpose. No one's actual beliefs are consistent and comprehensive. Everyone has at least some contradictory beliefs, and no one has an opinion on every claim with a truth value. Consider the claim that there is a prime number of blades of grass in my back yard. Both it and its denial fit about equally well with the rest of what I believe. Nevertheless, one is true and the other is false.

Blanshard's strategy is to appeal instead to the "ideal" set of beliefs, rather than anyone's actual beliefs. That approach has two main problems.

First, we need an account of what makes a set of beliefs *ideal*. It can't be just a matter of the set's internal features, such as its coherence and comprehensiveness, because conflicting sets of beliefs can rate equally well on that score. But if we look to some external feature of the set of beliefs, such as corresponding to the way things really are, or being the unique comprehensive set of *true* beliefs, then we have given up on the coherence theory of truth altogether.

As Bertrand Russell (1912) pointed out, coherentists have no non-arbitrary way of singling out one system of beliefs as the "ideal" system. Suppose MILKY is the ideal system, and so it is true that MILKY is the ideal system. Given coherentism, all it can mean to say it is true that MILKY is the ideal system in that case is:

(8) 'MILKY is the ideal system' fits with MILKY.

But so what? 'DRY is the ideal system' fits with DRY just as well, after all. The mere fact that MILKY is ideal by its own lights is nothing special about it, and it is no sound basis for picking MILKY out as the one system of belief, among the infinity of equally coherent and comprehensive systems, that constitutes truth. The trouble, as Russell points out, is that coherentism does not leave room for the world itself to play a role in determining what is true.

Another problem with the appeal to an "ideal system" of belief is that it renders the first premise of Blanshard's argument implausible. Though there may be good reasons to think testing a belief for truth requires checking how well it fits with what we actually believe, the first premise of Blanshard's argument says that we are seeing how well it fits with some *ideal* set of beliefs. That ideal set of beliefs would have to contain beliefs we do not actually hold, and it would exclude any of our actual beliefs that are false. Even if it is plausible that we test claims by seeing how they fit with what we do believe, the first premise of Blanshard's argument claims that we test claims by seeing how they fit with things we don't believe, and that seems wrong.

It appears that Blanshard's argument for coherentism must have at least one false premise. Much of what we actually believe is false. So, truth must be something other than just passing the test of fitting with what we actually believe. If our test for truth is a matter of seeing how well beliefs cohere with our actual beliefs, then, the second premise of the argument is false: truth is not the same as passing *that* test. If we appeal to an ideal set of beliefs, such that fitting with it is enough to constitute truth, then the first premise of the argument turns out to be false. We don't test claims for truth by seeing how well they fit with things we don't believe. If our tests for truth amount to checking the coherence of beliefs with one another, the only plausible option is that the beliefs in question are beliefs we actually hold.

These problems indicate that the coherence theory of truth is not viable, but coherentism is not the only epistemic theory of truth. Pragmatic theories offer an alternative.

4.4   Pragmatic Theories of Truth

Pragmatism is a set of views closely associated with the American philosophers C. S. Peirce and William James, as well as some others. One of its distinguishing features is its theory of concepts. As Peirce put it:

> consider what effects, which might have practical bearing, we conceive the object of our conception to have. Then our conception of these effects is the whole of our conception of the object. (1878/1982, p. 88)

In other words, the meaning of a concept consists in the practical difference it makes for the concept to apply to something or not. A practical difference is a difference in how things would turn out for our actions.

Peirce illustrates this idea with the concept of *hardness*. If we suppose something is hard, we are supposing that various ways we might interact with it will turn out in certain ways. Attempts to scratch it with many other substances will fail; it won't crumble to dust when we touch it; etc. On Peirce's view, such "practical" consequences of being hard exhaust our concept of hardness.

Peirce thinks we can account for the concept of truth in a similar way. What are the practical consequences of a claim's being true? Peirce's answer is that, if we were to investigate the claim diligently and open-mindedly, eventually we would all come to accept it. "The opinion which is fated to be ultimately agreed to by all who investigate," he writes (Peirce 1878/1982, p. 97), "is what we mean by truth, and the object represented in this opinion is the real." The point is not that truth is what we all as a matter of fact believe, but rather what we *would* believe at the ideal end of all inquiry, when we had investigated everything thoroughly and our opinions have converged to a consensus that is free from doubt.

Like Blanshard, Peirce works from the supposition that truth is a matter of passing our tests for truth. For Peirce, though, those tests are embodied in the ongoing practice of scientific inquiry, and passing them means winning acceptance, in the ideal long run, of all those who investigate the claim scientifically. Peirce grounds the idea that truth is a matter of passing our tests in the more general idea that the meaning of *any* concept is a matter of the practical difference it makes for concept to apply to something. To investigate a claim scientifically is to see whether our actions really do turn out the way they would if the claim were true. We can thus put together an argument for Peirce's pragmatic theory of truth that is similar to Blanshard's argument for coherentism:

(9) Since the meaning of 'true' is exhausted by the practical consequences of a claim's being true, and the practical

consequence of a claim's being true is just that it will pass our tests, all there is to truth is passing our tests for truth.

(10) For a claim to pass our tests for truth is for it to be one that everyone would believe at the ideal end of inquiry, when it had been investigated thoroughly and opinions had converged to a consensus free from doubt.

(11) Therefore, for a claim to be true is for it to be one everyone would believe at the ideal end of inquiry.

The Peircean pragmatist position appeals to the ideal "end of inquiry." Such an appeal might be necessary to avoid the absurd consequence that the truth changes whenever scientific consensus does. Before Copernicus, the consensus among inquirers was that the sun moves around the stationary earth once a day. Later, the consensus was that the earth rotates on its axis and orbits the sun. The appeal to the ideal "end of inquiry" allows us to avoid saying that, when the scientific consensus changed, the motions of the earth and sun also changed.

Nevertheless, it is hard to make sense of exactly what the ideal end of inquiry might be, and it is especially hard to see why we should imagine that, if inquiry were just carried out for long enough by enough open-minded people, their opinions would ultimately converge on a consensus. That is especially so in the case of truths that are very remote in space or time. Did the last dinosaur chip a tooth ten minutes before dying? Presumably, it did or it did not, but there is no reason to think any amount of inquiry could determine which or lead to consensus.

Peirce was aware of this problem, but his response to it was weak. He claimed it was

unphilosophical to suppose that, with regard to any given question (which has any clear meaning), investigation would not bring forth a solution of it, if it were carried far enough. (Peirce 1878/1982, p. 98)

Even if "unphilosophicalness" is reason to think a view is mistaken, it would be equally "unphilosophical" simply to assume that, if ever investigators put their efforts to any question for long enough, they will always be able to resolve it.

William James's version of the pragmatic theory of truth differs from Peirce's, but it draws on the same idea that the meaning of the concept of truth consists of the practical consequences that follow on a claim's being true. James sees the practical consequences of truth differently from Peirce, though. On James's view, 'truth' is a label we apply to beliefs because we have found those beliefs to *work*, in the sense that we succeed when we act on them. He writes,

> "The true" is only the expedient in the way of our thinking, just as "the right" is only the expedient in the way of our behaving. Expedient in almost any fashion; and expedient in the long run and on the whole, of course; for what meets expediently all the experience in sight won't necessarily meet all farther experiences equally satisfactorily. (James 1907a)

James's view avoids appealing to the consensus of investigators at the end of inquiry, but it faces serious problems of its own. A common objection to the view is that, quite bluntly, false beliefs are often expedient, and true beliefs are often bad for us. So truth can't be expedience.

Consider Stephen Stich's case of poor Harry, whose plane crashed in the mountains, killing all aboard (Stich 1990). Harry's true belief about when the plane would take off was, "in the long run and on the whole," not expedient for him at all. It was good enough to get him on the plane, but he would have been better off missing the flight. Even if, as a rule, we're more likely to accomplish our goals by acting on true beliefs than false ones, it is a mistake to equate truth with expediency in the way James does.

4.5 Epistemic Theories and the Equivalence Principle

In their own rights, neither coherentism nor pragmatism seems plausible as a theory of truth. We can illustrate their failures by way of the Equivalence Schema, 'It is true that _, if, and only if, _'. If coherentism were correct, then we should be able to substitute 'fits with a coherent and comprehensive system of belief' for 'is true' in the schema, to get:

(12)   The claim that _ fits with a coherent and comprehensive system of beliefs if, and only if, _.

And we should expect the instances of that schema to come out correct.

Thanks to the problem of alternative coherent systems, it is fairly easy to come up with incorrect instances of the schema. Anything logically consistent is part of *some* coherent and comprehensive system of belief. Thus, if we fill the blanks with 'Smith owns a Chevrolet' and 'Smith does not own a Chevrolet', then we would have:

(13)   The claim that Smith owns a Chevrolet fits with a coherent and comprehensive system of beliefs if, and only if, Smith owns a Chevrolet.

and

(14)   The claim that Smith does not own a Chevrolet fits with a coherent and comprehensive system of beliefs if, and only if, Smith does not own a Chevrolet.

Since both the 'Smith owns a Chevrolet' and 'Smith does not own a Chevrolet' fit with coherent and comprehensive systems of belief, we could then conclude that *both* Smith owns a Chevrolet *and* Smith does not own a Chevrolet. Coherentism, in conjunction with the Equivalence Schema, thus entails a large number of contradictions.

Pragmatism's main problems are similar. The Peircean pragmatist version of the Equivalence Schema is:

(15)   The claim that _ would be the consensus of investigators at the end of inquiry if, and only if, _.

But so long as there are things that no amount of inquiry will be able to discover, the "if" direction fails. And if it is possible for investigators to make a mistake, even as they converge on consensus in the ideal long run, the "only if" direction fails as well.

The Jamesian version of the Equivalence Schema is:

(16) The claim that _ is expedient to believe if, and only if, _.

The counterexamples are obvious. One instance of the schema is this:

(17) The claim that Harry's flight takes off at 8:15 a.m. is expedient to believe if, and only if, Harry's flight takes off at 8:15 a.m.

Suppose Harry's flight will crash in the mountains, killing all aboard. Then it is not expedient to believe the flight takes off at 8:15 a.m. But, it follows from the above instance of the Equivalence Schema that Harry's plane takes off at 8:15 only if it is expedient to believe it does. We can thus conclude that, since the plane will crash, it does not take off at 8:15!

4.6 Epistemic Theories, Realism, and Anti-Realism

Combining an epistemic theory of truth – especially Peircean pragmatism – with a form of anti-realism could mitigate some of its problems. Recall that anti-realism is the view that truth is mind-dependent, specifically in the sense that everything true is knowable. On the Peircean pragmatist view, for a claim to be true is for it to be what the community of investigators would agree on at the ideal end of inquiry. Clearly, this view is committed to the view that everything true is knowable.

Anti-realism gives Peircean pragmatists an option for dealing with objections concerning unknowable claims – such as the claim that the last dinosaur chipped a tooth ten minutes before dying. Given anti-realism, these are not counterexamples to the pragmatist view of truth; they are claims that lack truth values altogether.

In general, epistemic theories of truth will be committed to anti-realism. This is because they identify truth with passing our tests for truth, and only knowable claims can pass those tests. There are two important consequences of this fact.

First, it means that any objections to anti-realism, such as those discussed in Chapter 2, are automatically also objections to epistemic theories of the nature of truth. Anti-realism, recall, runs into problems both because it counts some claims that do seem to have truth values as having no truth value at all, and also because it requires us to give up on such principles of logic as the law of excluded middle (i.e., "*P* or Not-*P*"). Moreover, it faces the Paradox of Knowability, the implausible result that, if all truths are knowable, all truths are in fact known.

Second, and conversely, it means realists will have to look elsewhere for a theory of truth's nature. They will need a theory of truth that does not tie it so closely to knowledge or our tests for truth. In the next chapter, we will look at a family of theories of truth that are meant to be especially well suited to the realist outlook. But we should also keep in mind what one of the original motivations for epistemic theories of truth was: that unless there is a close connection between truth and knowledge, skepticism poses a serious threat.

4.7   Epistemic Theories and the Value of Truth

Despite the other problems epistemic theories of truth face, they do especially well when it comes to the value of truth. In fact, such epistemicists as William James seem motivated more by the idea that it is good to believe what is true than by anything else. "The true is the name of whatever proves itself to be good in the way of belief," James writes, and he argues that for a belief to be good is, in practical terms, for it to be expedient or helpful in getting us what we want. His account builds value right into the nature of truth (James 1907b).

Coherence theories and Peircean theories are less explicit about the value of truth, but it is not hard to see how one might explain the value of truth in their terms. We start with the idea that our beliefs are accountable to rules of justification. We are doing something wrong when our beliefs are not justified, and we are doing something right when they are. What makes a belief justified? Epistemologists have offered a wide array of theories, but we can see the sorts of things coherentists and Peircean pragmatists are apt to say. Coherentists will claim that beliefs are justified in virtue of their connections to one another. When they form a suitably coherent body of belief, they are justified, and beliefs that do not cohere with the rest of what one believes are unjustified. Peircean pragmatists, on the other hand, will emphasize the role of testing our beliefs against experience in their justification. We put our beliefs to the test by determining their practical consequences and seeing if those consequences obtain. As they pass that test, beliefs increase in justification.

If truth is just an idealization or elaboration of justification, it is easy to see how truth could be a normative property. For a person's belief to be justified is for it to be rationally permissible for her to believe that in her circumstances. Truth, then, would be an idealization or elaboration of a kind of rational permissibility. It would be, essentially, a variety of goodness or correctness.

Epistemicists need not take a position on whether truth is intrinsically, instrumentally, finally, or telically valuable, or whether caring about truth is constitutively valuable. If they think of justified belief as intrinsically valuable, they are apt to think the same of truth. And if they think of truth as the aim of belief, as they are quite likely to do, then they should be able to give an account of truth as finally valuable, since final value is just a matter of being aimed at by rational beings. This is an advantage for the epistemic approach. It is consistent with a wide array of explanations of truth's value, and it provides a clear explanation of why truth would appear to have some forms of value. We hold our beliefs accountable to rules of justification, and being true is just a matter of being justified especially (or ideally) well.

4.8 Final Assessment of Epistemic Theories

Given the problems of coherentism and pragmatism about truth, one might be attracted to a more generic epistemic theory of truth. Such a generic epistemic theory would say that a belief is true if, and only if, it is justified or warranted by the evidence available to the believer. A generic epistemic theory has serious disadvantages.

First, different people are justified or warranted in believing different things. Such a generic epistemic theory then amounts to a close relative of subjectivist relativism: whatever you are justified in believing is true for you, and whatever I am justified in believing is true for me. This kind of subjectivism is untenable. Take the claim that there is milk in the refrigerator, and suppose you have good evidence it is true (as you are standing there looking into the refrigerator) while I have good evidence it is not (as you, standing there looking into the refrigerator, have just told me there is no milk in there). It is absurd to suppose that it is true for you that there is milk in the refrigerator but false for me. The milk is there or it isn't, and its location does not depend on what anyone is justified in believing.

A second problem is implicit in the first. We want a theory of truth that will satisfy the Equivalence Principle and thus deliver as many of the T-biconditionals as we can get. One such T-biconditional is:

(18) 'There is milk in the refrigerator' is true if, and only if, there is milk in the refrigerator.

But if truth is warranted belief, we would then have this:

(19) The information available to one warrants believing that there is milk in the refrigerator if, and only if, there is milk in the refrigerator.

That biconditional seems to get things wrong, though. One could be warranted in believing there is milk in the refrigerator even though none is there. (Perhaps the last person to drink any put back an empty carton). And there could be milk in the refrigerator even though one is not warranted in believing there is. In general, warrant might be a good sign or indicator of truth, but it cannot be what truth is.

Epistemic theories of truth are ultimately unsatisfactory. They are supported by weak arguments, suffer from internal problems, fail the Equivalence Principle's test, and inherit all the problems of anti-realism. Nevertheless, it is worth taking note that they are consistent with a number of views on truth's value, and they make truth's role as a norm of belief clearly explicable. So, in rejecting epistemic theories, we can also see the importance of the challenge other theories of truth's nature will face: How can we account for the value of truth without abandoning the Equivalence Principle and realism?

Further Reading

Blanshard (1939) lays out the case for coherentism fairly clearly, and Bertrand Russell (1912) outlines some classic objections to epistemic theories. F. H. Bradley (1914, Chapters V and VII) argues for coherentism, particularly against the correspondence theory (see Chapter V), and Russell (1906) criticizes a view in line with Bradley's. Dale Dorsey (2006) develops in great detail W. V. Quine's (1981) suggestion that ethics requires a coherence theory of truth. For conceptions of coherence that relax the requirement of consistency, see Priest (2006) and Lynch (2009b, Chapter 8).

The classic source for Peirce's pragmatic theory of truth is "How to Make Our Ideas Clear" (1878). Hilary Putnam (1981) elaborates an understanding of truth in terms of what we would be justified in believing in ideal circumstances, which is similar in some respects to Peirce's pragmatist theory of truth. William James outlines his version of pragmatism, and its view of truth, in (1907a).

As usual, the online *Stanford Encyclopedia of Philosophy* has several articles related to the topics of this chapter, with extensive references. See especially "Truth" (Glanzberg 2009), "Pragmatism" (Hookway 2010) and "The Coherence Theory of Truth" (Young 2013).

5

Correspondence Theories of Truth

5.1 The Idea that Truth Depends on the World

Epistemic theories of truth err in giving reality too small a role in determining which claims are true and which are false. The truth or falsity of the claim that snow is white, for example, should be up to the snow, not how the claim fits with other claims or what we believe about snow. So-called "correspondence" theories of truth take this idea very seriously. They aim to explain truth as a relation between claims, on the one hand, and the world, on the other. Such theories have been the traditional allies of realism and the traditional rivals of epistemic theories.

This chapter addresses three kinds of correspondence theory: classical correspondence theories, causal correspondence theories, and truthmaker theories. We will evaluate each view along the same lines as we evaluated epistemic theories of truth: in terms of its intrinsic advantages and disadvantages, its compatibility with the Equivalence Principle, its consequences for realism, and its ability to make sense of the value of truth.

5.2 Classical Correspondence Theories

The central idea of correspondence theories is that truth is the correspondence (or "fit" or "agreement") of a claim to reality. There are, however, several different ways to understand that idea.

For example, one might understand 'corresponds to reality' as just another expression for 'true', without giving the expression any deep metaphysical significance. A coherentist thus might say that truth is correspondence to reality, while 'corresponding to reality' means being part of a suitably coherent system. Or a pragmatist might say that corresponding to reality is being destined to be agreed on at the ideal limit of inquiry. This is not what correspondence theorists have in mind.

Correspondence theorists take 'corresponds to reality', 'corresponds to the facts', 'fits the facts', 'agrees with the world', and similar expressions very seriously. They construe truth as a *relational property*, a property something has in virtue of its relationship to something else. To explain the nature of such a property, one must explain that relationship.

Some examples can make this a bit clearer. Consider the property of *being a spouse*. To be a spouse is to be married to someone else. It is a relational property. The property of *being a sibling* is also relational. To be a sibling is to have the same parents as someone else. Families are not the only place where relational properties are found. *Being the biggest piece of cake* is a relational property. To be the biggest piece of cake is to be a piece of cake that is larger than all the other pieces of cake. To be biggest is not just to be a certain size, but for that size to be *larger than* the size of other things.

A theory of the nature of a relational property needs to do two things. First, it should say what the *relata* of the relation are – what sorts of things bear the relation to what other sorts of things. Second, it should say what it means for those things to be related in that way.

Consider *being a spouse* again. To be a spouse is to bear the *married to* relation to another person. The relata of the *married to* relation are people, and for two people to be married is for them to have met certain culturally instituted conditions.

Now consider *being a driver*. To be a driver is to bear the *drives* relation to a vehicle. The relata of the *drives* relation are people (who do the driving) on the one hand, and vehicles (which are driven) on the other. For a person to drive a vehicle is for her to direct the vehicle's movement. *Being a driver* is thus a relational property that people can have in virtue of directing the movement of vehicles.

According to correspondence theories, truth is also a relational property. Claims are true in virtue of bearing a "correspondence" relation to something else, though theories differ on what they take the relata of the correspondence relation to be, and on how they characterize the relation's nature. In general, though, these theories construe truth as a property claims have in virtue of how they are related to whatever they are *about*.

According to *classical* correspondence theories, the relata of the correspondence relation are claims, on the one hand, and *facts* on the other. To be true is to bear the correspondence relation to a fact. These theories thus owe an account of what facts are, as well as an account of what it means for a claim to correspond to one.

In ordinary talk, we use the word 'fact' in several different ways, but many of those uses differ from what classical correspondence theorists have in mind. For example, we sometimes use 'fact' to mean 'true claim' or 'true proposition', as in:

(1)   Alice stated several relevant facts about the economy.

If we thought of facts as true claims, then we might think of "corresponding" to a fact as a simply *being* a fact. But classical correspondence theorists think of truth as arising from the relation of a claim to the world, not to itself. This isn't the sense of 'fact' they have in mind.

Sometimes, we distinguish "facts" from "opinions," with the idea that facts are indisputable or uncontroversial items of knowledge, while opinions are beliefs that might be based on facts, but are disputable, controversial, or uncertain. Thus we might say it is a fact that the GDP has been declining for the past six months, but reasonable people might have different opinions about what the best response to the situation might be. People sometimes talk about "facts and figures" as data on which theories or beliefs might be based. In these senses, 'fact' still refers to a certain kind of claim, and it is not what classical correspondence theorists have in mind.

What classical correspondence theorists *do* have in mind is the sense of 'fact' that means *a way the world is* or *a way things are*. They might follow Ludwig Wittgenstein in thinking of the world itself as "the totality of facts" (Wittgenstein 1922, Sect. 1.1). The classical correspondence idea is that, for any true claim, there is a corresponding way the world is, and the claim is true because the world is that way. That leads to the following simple version of the classical correspondence theory:

(2) A claim is true if, and only if, there is a fact corresponding to that claim.

Two further questions arise from (2). First, how are we to account for *falsehood* as well as *truth*? Second, what makes a given fact correspond (or not) to a given claim?

A natural answer to the second question is that a claim *represents* the world as being a certain way. The fact corresponding to a claim is then whatever way the claim represents the world as being. For example, the claim that there are marsupials in Australia represents the world as containing marsupials in Australia. The fact corresponding to that claim is the fact that there are marsupials in Australia.

But now consider this false claim:

(3) All reptiles bear their young alive.

If we think of true claims as representing facts, the problem is to say what *false* claims represent. They can't represent facts. If (3) represented a fact, then there would be such a thing as *the fact that all reptiles bear their young alive*, and so (3) would be true, not false. On the other hand, it seems equally mistaken to say that false claims represent nothing at all. Doing so comes at the price of losing two important distinctions. Take the following false claim:

(4)   Some squares have only three sides.

We should be able to distinguish what (3) represents from what (4) represents. But if neither of them represents anything, that distinction disappears. We also seem to lose the distinction between meaningful, but false, claims such as (3) and (4), and meaningless pseudo-claims such as Lewis Carroll's:

(5)   The mome raths outgrabe.

Neither (3), (4), nor (5) represents a fact, but we still need to say something about what (3) and (4) *do* represent. They are meaningful, and so they seem to represent *something*, while (5), being meaningless, does not represent anything at all.

What (3) represents is not a fact, but apparently it could have been. The world could have been such that all reptiles bear their young alive. So, it seems, (3) represents not a way the world *is*, but a way the world *could have been*.

Such considerations have led some philosophers to posit *states of affairs* as the things claims represent. Some, but not all, states of affairs "obtain." When a state of affairs obtains, it is a fact. So, for the fact that snow is white to exist is just for the state of affairs of snow's being white to obtain. The claim that snow is white represents the state of affairs of snow's being white, and, since that state of affairs obtains, it is a fact. That is the sense in which 'snow is white' corresponds to a fact.

Some states of affairs do not obtain. One non-obtaining state of affairs is that all reptiles bear their young alive. That state of affairs, which (3) represents, is not a fact. What makes (3) false is that the state of affairs it represents is not a fact. A meaningless pseudo-claim such as (5), in contrast, does not represent any state of affairs at all. That is why it cannot be true or false. Representing no state of affairs at all, it neither represents a state of affairs that obtains nor represents one that does not obtain.

Some states of affairs are *necessary*; they are bound to obtain no matter what. One example of such a state of affairs is the state of affairs that all bachelors are unmarried. Other states of affairs are impossible. They exist, but they could not possibly obtain. An example of an impossible state of affairs is the state of affairs that some squares have only three sides. That state of affairs does not – and cannot – obtain, but it does *exist*, and claim (4) above represents it.

If we think of claims as representing states of affairs, we still might ask what makes a claim represent one state of affairs rather than another. For example, why does 'Snow is white' represent the state of affairs that snow is white, rather than the state of affairs that sulfur is yellow? And what makes (3) represent a different state of affairs from (4), which is equally false?

This problem arises whether we think of claims as propositions or sentences. If claims are sentences, it is the problem of what makes a sentence represent the world as one way rather than another. If claims are propositions, we might think of each claim as representing a certain state of affairs *essentially*, for the identity of a proposition depends on what state of affairs it represents. The claim that grass is green could not possibly represent the state of affairs that snow is white, for example. Even given that it is essential to a claim to represent a certain state of affairs, though, we still have not explained precisely what the representation relation amounts to.

A natural and popular move is to take very seriously the fact that, in saying what fact or state of affairs the claim that *p* represents, we seem bound to refer to it as the fact or state of affairs *that p*. For example, the claim that snow is white represents the state of affairs that snow is white. The claim that the sun is a chariot represents the state of affairs that the sun is a chariot. The claim that Bob will attend the party only if Carol is there represents the state of affairs that Bob will attend the party only if Carol is there. And so on. True claims seem to give us pictures of facts. The repetition of the '*p*' part in 'the fact that *p*' and the 'the claim that *p*' is significant. It shows us that there is an isomorphism – i.e., a sameness of structure – between claims and states of affairs. That isomorphism enables claims to represent states of affairs by picturing them. When the state of affairs pictured obtains, it is a fact and the claim is true. When it does not obtain, the claim is false.

Classical correspondence theories enjoy some important advantages. Their most significant advantage is that they have a powerful intuition on their side. That is the intuition that, when a claim is true, it is true because it is related to the world (and, in particular, the chunk of the world the claim is about) in a special way. When a claim is false, the world isn't the way the claim says it is. Aristotle expressed this intuition in the passage from *Metaphysics* quoted in Chapter 1:

> To say of what is not that it is, or of what is that it is not, is false, while to say of what is that it is, and of what is not that it is not, is true.

Classical correspondence theories do justice to the idea that a claim's truth or falsehood depends on two things: first, what way the claim says the world is, and second, whether the world is that way. These theories manage to give the external world precisely the role in determining what is true that epistemic theories fail to give it.

Nevertheless, classical correspondence theories face some serious problems. One problem has to do with the nature of the correspondence relation itself. We might have an intuitive grasp of how 'The cat is on the mat' corresponds to a state of affairs in the world involving a certain cat being located in a certain place relative to a certain mat. But when it comes to some claims about mathematics, morality, and possibility, things get much less clear. Take these three, claims, for example:

(6)   The square root of 100 is 10.
(7)   It was wrong for Jesse James to shoot John Sheets.
(8)   Gandhi never killed anyone, but he could have.

On the classical correspondence view, each of these true claims must correspond to a fact. But what does it mean for (6), (7), or (8) to do that?

Imagine that correspondence is isomorphism. Claims correspond to states of affairs in virtue of sharing a structure with them. When those states of affairs obtain, the claims are true. The trouble is that reality doesn't come in sentence-shaped chunks. Sentences aren't pictures, and they are not isomorphic with what they are about in any philosophically significant way. After all, 'Snow is white' and 'Grass is green' are much more structurally similar to one another than either is to the whiteness of snow or the greenness of grass.

As J. L. Austin (1950) argued, to think of correspondence as isomorphism is to be misled by an illusion of language. The *expressions* we use to identify claims and to identify facts are similar in structure; we talk about *the claim that snow is white* and *the fact that snow is white*. It does not follow, however, that the claim and the fact themselves share that structure. Moreover, to suppose they do share a structure, we must adopt an implausible view of the world as a great collection of what P. F. Strawson is held to have disparaged as "sentence-shaped objects" (Rorty 1995).

As we try to get clearer and clearer about what those sentence-shaped objects are, they become less and less plausible. Take the state of affairs that the mat is something under the cat. Is that the same as the state of affairs that the cat is on the mat? The structure of the claim *that the cat is on the mat* seems to be different from the structure of the claim *that the mat is something under the cat*. But if those are two different claims, with two different structures, we apparently also need two differently structured facts for them to correspond to: the fact that the cat is on the mat, and the fact that the mat is something under the cat. A similar problem applies to (6). Is the fact that 10 is the square root of 100 the same fact, or a different one, from the fact that $10 \times 10 = 100$, or the fact that $5 \times 2 \times 2 \times 5 = 99 + 1$? If they are the same, then it looks as though isomorphism is not what makes claims represent states of affairs. If they are different, facts appear to be *so* sentence-like that it is hard to see them as anything other than artifacts of our language, mere "shadows cast by words" (Pears 1951).

A second problem for classical correspondence theories is similar to the first. The classical correspondence view seems committed to an overcrowded and redundant ontology. (A theory's "ontology" is the collection of things the theory says exist.) Not only is there the fact that the cat is on the mat, but the fact that the mat is something under the cat, the fact that 10 is the square root of 100, and the facts that $10 \times 10 = 100$ and $5 \times 2 \times 2 \times 5 = 99 + 1$. If claims correspond to states of affairs, we need states of affairs for them to correspond to, and we need a lot of them. We need ways the world is, for true claims to correspond to. We also need ways the world *isn't*, for false claims to correspond to. We need the non-obtaining state of affairs to which 'Triangles have four sides' corresponds, and we also need the obtaining state of affairs to which 'Triangles do not have four sides' corresponds. It would be good to cut down on the ontological overcrowding and find a way to let fewer entities do the necessary theoretical work.

Another kind of ontological overcrowding comes from the mysteriousness of some of the facts and states of affairs classical correspondence theories posit. It is not at all clear what it means to say that one of reality's constituents is the fact that 10 is the square root of 100, or that it was wrong for Jesse James to shoot John Sheets, or that Gandhi never killed anyone but could have. Even if we can think of the world as dividing into chunks that involve the locations of cats and the colors of vegetation and precipitation, it is much more mysterious what chunk of reality any of these other kinds of fact might be.

The supposition that there are non-obtaining states of affairs faces a potentially worse problem of the same sort. Perhaps we can make sense of what it means for there to be an obtaining state of affairs, and perhaps we can think of the world as built out of obtaining states of affairs. But what is a state of affairs that does not obtain, and what does it mean to say that a certain state of affairs *exists*, though it does not obtain? Consider, for example, the state of affairs that Abraham Lincoln was born on the moon. Our only grasp of the idea that it is a real, but non-obtaining, state of affairs, seems to come by way of the idea that 'Abraham Lincoln was born on the moon' is a meaningful, but false sentence. That is unhelpful, though, if our aim is to explain falsehood in terms of the existence of non-obtaining states of affairs. Until we can understand what non-obtaining states of affairs are supposed to be, without presupposing an understanding of truth and falsehood, they are an odd and unwelcome addition to our ontology.

5.3 From Classical to Causal Correspondence

The two greatest challenges for the classical correspondence view are, first, to give a satisfactory account of what facts and states of affairs are and, second, to give a satisfactory account of what it means for a claim to correspond to one. Since the 1970s, so-called "causal correspondence" theories of truth have aimed to resolve both problems at once. Their general strategy has two prongs. First, they define truth for sentences in terms of the relation of *reference* or *designation*. The word 'snow' refers to something in the world, namely snow. Likewise, 'white' refers to the property of whiteness, and 'Abraham Lincoln' refers to Abraham Lincoln. Second, they adopt a causal theory of reference. Such a theory says that 'snow' refers to snow, for example, in virtue of a special causal relationship between snow and our usage of the word 'snow'.

The first prong – defining truth in terms of designation – draws on crucially important work in mathematical logic by Alfred Tarski. The details of Tarski's project are too technical for present purposes, so here I will outline a highly simplified version of it. (Readers of Tarski might find it instructive to note the ways in which this version differs from his, and why his more technical apparatus are necessary.)

Some terms function as names – 'snow' names snow, 'Abraham Lincoln' names Abraham Lincoln, 'the Grand Canyon' names the Grand Canyon, and so on. Let us say that such terms "designate" the things they name. We will call them "singular terms." Other terms, known as "general terms," are used not to pick out or name individuals but to pick out *properties* that individuals might or might not have. For example, 'white' picks out the property of whiteness, 'lived in the nineteenth century' picks out the property of having lived in the nineteenth century, and 'deep' picks out the property of deepness. Let us also say general terms designate the properties they pick out.

We can construct some simple sentences by combining these two kinds of terms. For example, we can combine 'snow' and 'white' (along with the grammatically necessary 'is') to form the sentence 'Snow is white.' We can also combine 'lived in the nineteenth century' with 'Abraham Lincoln' to form the sentence 'Abraham Lincoln lived in the nineteenth century', and so on. Sentences like that are called "atomic."

We can make more complicated sentences out of atomic ones. For example, we can negate an atomic sentence to say 'Snow is not white' or 'The Grand Canyon did not live in the nineteenth century'. We can also combine them with 'and', 'or', and 'if ... then ...'. We can even make sentences without using names at all, by using so-called "quantifiers" like 'something' and 'everything' along with general terms. Thus we can say 'Everything is white' and 'Something lived in the nineteenth century.' Plus, we can make complex general terms out of simpler ones by using similar devices. Along with 'white' and 'deep', for example, we have such general terms as 'white or deep', 'lived in the eighteenth or nineteenth century', 'spoiled if it's been left out of the refrigerator for a week', and 'not spoiled'.

There is no limit to how much we can combine and recombine sentences or general terms to make ever more complex ones. No matter how complicated two sentences are, we can make a more complicated one by combining them with 'and', 'or', or 'if ... then', and we can negate them as well. The same goes for general terms.

We have now identified two sorts of general terms – simple ones and complex ones. We have also identified seven types of sentences:

atomic sentences, which combine a singular term and a general term,

universals, which combine 'everything' and a general term, and

existentials, which combine 'something' and a general term,

negations of sentences,

conjunctions, which combine two sentences with 'and',

disjunctions, which combine two sentences with 'or',

conditionals, which combine two sentences with 'if ... then'.

Now, let us say that an object "satisfies" a general term when it has the property the general term designates. Since snow has the property of being white, it satisfies the term 'white'. Since Abraham Lincoln has the property of having lived in the nineteenth century, he satisfies 'lived in the nineteenth century', and since the Grand Canyon does not have the property of being located on the moon, it does not satisfy 'is located on the moon'. Let us suppose that all sentences are of one of the types listed above. Then we can define truth in the following way:

(9) A sentence is true if and only if either:
   (a) it is atomic, and the object the singular term designates satisfies the general term, or
   (b) it is universal, and everything satisfies the general term, or
   (c) it is existential, and something satisfies the general term, or
   (d) it is a negation, and the sentence negated is false, or
   (e) it is a conjunction, and both the sentences conjoined are true, or
   (f) it is a disjunction, and either of the sentences composing it is true, or
   (g) it is a conditional, and if the sentence after 'if' is true, then so is the sentence after 'then'.

Although the word 'true' appears in clauses (d) through (g), the definition is not circular. This is because all negations, conjunctions, disjunctions, and conditionals are, ultimately, built up out of atomic, universal, and existential claims, and truth for those claims has been defined without making any use of 'true'.

This way of defining truth preserves the idea that truth is a matter of how our claims are related to the world. Whether a sentence is true or not ultimately depends on which objects in the world satisfy (or fail to satisfy) which general terms. But it gets by without introducing facts as a new category of reality. To satisfy a general term is to have the property it designates. The truth of a sentence thus hinges on what it means and which objects have which properties.

Although truth thus depends on a claim's connection to reality, that connection is not a matter of corresponding to metaphysically suspicious entities such as "facts" or "states of affairs."

Not only does this approach do without metaphysically suspicious facts, it does without the equally suspicious relation of "correspondence." Instead of understanding truth directly as a relation of corresponding with facts, the theory treats the relation of designation as what matters to truth. Truth in general depends on which objects have which properties. The truth of a particular claim, though, depends on whether the objects its singular terms designate (or, in the case of universals or existentials, all objects or some objects, respectively) have the properties its general terms designate. We don't need a theory of the correspondence relation so long as we have a theory of the designation (or "reference") relation.

That is what the second part of the causal correspondence theory aims to provide. According to it, the nature of reference is causal. For a term to designate an object or property is for it to be causally connected to that object or property in the right way. Why, for example, does our word 'snow' designate snow, rather than grass or Abraham Lincoln? According to the causal theory of reference, it is because our uses of the word 'snow' are caused in a certain way by snow, but they aren't caused in that way by grass or by Abraham Lincoln.

Philosophers have offered several different versions of the causal theory of reference, each aimed at elucidating some aspect of what it might mean for our uses of a word to be causally connected to an object or property "in the right way" to designate it. However the causal theory of reference gets worked out, though, it helps to eliminate the mystery of how a claim could correspond to reality. If we have a clear understanding of how terms designate objects and properties, there is no longer any need for a theory of correspondence, conceived as a relation between whole claims and facts. A theory of reference will explain the connection between sentences and the world, and it can suffice to yield a definition of truth.

5.4   Problems for Causal Correspondence

Though it manages to avoid some problems of the classical correspondence view, the causal correspondence theory faces its own difficulties. Some of them derive from its method of defining truth in terms of designation and satisfaction. Others derive from its commitment to a causal theory of reference. Both sets of problems are instances of what will be discussed as the "Scope Problem" later in this chapter.

Tarski's original work was not aimed at producing a causal correspondence theory of truth. Rather, it was Hartry Field (1972) who adapted Tarski's work, added a causal theory of reference to it, and first articulated a causal correspondence theory of truth. Tarski's project was, rather, to show how 'true sentence' could be defined for certain formal, mathematical languages. Indeed, it was important to Tarski that he *not* provide a definition of truth in general, but rather only showed how to define 'true in language *L*', for a mathematical language *L* with certain very specific properties. Among those properties were that every sentence of the language was of one of the seven types listed above, that complex general terms were created by way of combining general terms with 'and', 'or', 'not', and 'if … then' in much the same way that complex sentences are created, and that the language not include resources for talking about the designation or satisfaction of its own expressions.

The Tarskian approach to defining truth relies on the idea that the truth of a complex sentence depends only on the truth of its constituents or, at least, on which objects satisfy the simple general terms in the claim. That approach is adequate for the seven kinds of claim listed above, but there are complex claims that are not of those types. Here are some samples:

(10)   Jack went to the park because Bart was in the library.
(11)   The Grand Canyon could not have been created by aliens from Alpha Centauri.
(12)   Abraham Lincoln should not have suspended *habeas corpus* during the American Civil War.

if we know that Jack satisfies 'went to the park' and atisfies 'was in the library', that's not enough informa-tion to tell us whether Jack went to the park *because* Bart was in the library. That the Grand Canyon *wasn't* created by aliens from Alpha Centauri does not tell us whether it *could* have been. Abraham Lincoln did suspend the right of *habeas corpus* during the Civil War, but that isn't enough to deter-mine whether he should not have done so.

Complex sentences involving 'because', 'should', 'could' and various other constructions pose a challenge to defini-tions of truth along Tarskian lines. It seems doubtful that we will ever be able to define truth for such sentences simply in terms of designation and satisfaction, but those sentences do seem to have truth values. The trouble is that, even when we have fixed the designations of the parts of the sentences, and even when we have settled what objects satisfy what general terms, that *still* is not enough to fix the truth values of the sentences. Whether (10) is true, for example, depends perhaps on something to do with Jack's state of mind when he went to the library, but that is not among the objects and properties designated by (10)'s terms.

Either (10) is true, or it is false. Likewise for (11) and (12). The Tarskian definition that undergirds the causal correspon-dence theory of truth is ill suited to dealing with claims such as these. At best, then, the causal correspondence theory fails to account for the full range of true and false claims. Such a failure is significant for a theory that purports to be a theory of the very nature of truth.

Even if we set the above problem aside, a further difficulty comes from the causal correspondence theory's application of a causal theory of reference. That theory says terms des-ignate the things they designate in virtue of being causally connected to them "in the right way." However, some terms appear to designate objects and properties without being causally connected to them in *any* way at all.

The main examples are terms for abstract objects, such as numbers, and moral properties, such as wrongness. The number twelve is an abstract object, very different from con-crete particular objects such as the cliffs of Dover, apples, and automobiles. Abstract objects do not exist in space in time. If we conducted a thorough and exhaustive census of the physical world, we would at no time happen upon the number twelve. Causation, though, is a strictly physical affair; abstract objects aren't involved in causal exchanges. The number twelve does not do anything, much less does it make anything happen. Nor can anything we do affect the number twelve in any way. Simply put, the number twelve isn't causally connected with anything at all. It's just the wrong sort of thing for that. Consequently, though, our uses of 'twelve' aren't causally connected to the number twelve in any way, much less in "the right way" to refer to it.

Similarly, the property of being morally wrong seems to be real enough – the Holocaust had it, loving your baby doesn't, and we have a term, 'wrong', that seems to designate it. On a causal theory of reference, 'wrong' designates this property because our use of the word is causally connected, in some special way, to wrongness in the world. Now consider some wrong action, such as a group of teens torturing a cat for fun (Harman 1977). We can tell a physical, causal story about exactly what happened and what its effects were. We can give a completely physical explanation of how that event causes people to say things such as 'That's wrong!' In telling that story, we would need to mention various things about events in the kids' brains, about what happened to the cat, and about photons bouncing off the cat, striking the retinas of onlookers, and triggering various brain events leading to utterances of 'That's wrong!', calls to the police, and the arrest of the kids. That physical, causal story, however, will never mention the *wrongness* of the action – not even in explaining the physical events of onlookers saying, "That's wrong!" What the kids did was wrong, but its wrongness isn't the sort of property that participates in causal exchanges. A causal theory of reference has trouble explaining how we could refer to such properties at all.

The causal correspondence theory of truth, then, runs into problems accounting for truth and falsity as they apply to abstract objects and their properties, claims about moral properties, and complex claims involving terms such as 'because' or 'could' or 'should'. A partisan of the theory could simply bite the bullet and deny that those are genuine claims with truth values at all. That would be a drastic move, though. It requires giving up the idea that anything truly is morally right or wrong, the idea that there are true claims about what could or would happen in certain circumstances, and the idea that there are mathematical truths. A move that gives up that much seems to be an ad hoc maneuver to save a favored theory, rather than the legitimate discovery that some of our cherished intuitions about truth are incompatible with what we have learned about truth's real nature.

5.5 Truthmakers

Both the classical and the causal correspondence theories are, in their ways, *semantic* theories of truth. That is, they draw a tight connection between truth and the meanings of claims. On a classical correspondence theory, correspondence is the relation between a claim and the state of affairs it is about, and the claim is true exactly when the state of affairs obtains.

The causal correspondence view, on the other hand, treats the meaning of a sentence as a function of what its components designate and how they are combined together, and it defines truth in terms of designation. The meanings of the singular and general terms in a sentence (that is, what they designate), along with the structure of the claim, determine how the world would have to be for the sentence to be true.

Some philosophers have recently explored the possibility of understanding truth in something like a correspondence way, but with a much looser connection between truth and meaning. The truth or falsity of a claim does depend, of course, on its meaning, but according to these new "truthmaker" theories, the project of understanding truth's nature is primarily a metaphysical project, rather than a semantic one.

A *truthmaker* for a claim is something that *makes the claim true*. The relevant sense of "making" here is that of necessitation. Consider the idea that snow's whiteness makes it true that snow is white. That is the idea that the existence of snow's whiteness necessitates the truth of the claim that snow is white: necessarily, if snow's whiteness exists, then the claim that snow is white is true. On the truthmaker account, the truth of a claim always requires the existence of something: if a claim is true, then there is something (a) that exists and (b) whose existence necessitates that the claim is true.

Truthmaker theorists often emphasize that the truthmaking relation need not be a one-to-one relation between claims and existing things. One claim might be made true by many things. For example, each and every mortal human might be a truthmaker for the claim that some humans are mortal. And a single thing could make many claims true. For example, the whiteness of snow might make true not only the claim that snow is white, but also the claim that either snow is white or grass is green and the claim that something is white. This is why truthmaker theories treat the issue of truth's nature separately from questions about meaning. 'Snow is white or squares have five sides' *means* that snow is white or squares have five sides, but it is *made true* by the whiteness of snow, not the (nonexistent) five-sidedness of squares.

One source of problems for the classical correspondence view was its need to treat correspondence as a relation between claims, on the one hand, and states of affairs – including non-obtaining states of affairs – on the other. How a state of affairs could exist without obtaining can seem mysterious, and the precise nature of the correspondence relation could seem equally mysterious. A truthmaker view can avoid these problems. What makes a claim true is the existence of something. And, because truthmaking is a matter of necessitation, we need only see that 'Some men are mortal' is true in virtue of the existence of some mortal men in order to understand the role the world plays in making 'Some men are mortal' true.

The truthmaker view can also avoid some of the difficulties of the causal correspondence theory. Consider the problem of accounting for the truth of a claim such as 'The window broke because Jack threw a brick at it.' A causal correspondence theory can have trouble with such a claim, since its truth depends on more than just the truth values and designations of its parts. A truthmaker theorist, on the other hand, might be able to account for the truth of 'The window broke because Jack threw a brick at it' by positing the existence of something that necessitates that the claim is true – for example, a causal connection between the breaking of the window and the throwing of the brick. Furthermore, the problems a causal correspondence theory has accounting for the truth of claims about abstract objects are of less concern for truthmaker theorists. It may be a hard question for the philosophy of language how we manage to refer to prime numbers, but when it comes to the truth of the claim that there are prime numbers greater than 2, a truthmaker theorist will point out that the claim has no shortage of truthmakers. Each of the infinitely many prime numbers greater than 2 makes it true that there are prime numbers greater than 2.

The truthmaker approach does suffer some problems of its own, though. Its two most significant problems are (a) that providing truthmakers for all true claims seems to require bloating our ontology in a strange way, and (b) that the theory may be no theory of the nature of truth at all.

Let's take the ontological problem first. Consider the claim that if Jack had gone to the party, he would have lost the game of *Monopoly*. On the truthmaker view, if this claim is true, something must exist that makes it true. This may not be much of a problem. Perhaps there is some complex of properties of *Monopoly*, the party, and Jack whose existence necessitates that Jack would have lost the game if he had been at the party. The real difficulty for truthmaker theories arises in connection with negative claims and with universal claims. For example, consider the claim that Jack does not own a horse, and suppose it is true. The truthmaker view requires that there exist something that makes that claim true. Although it is reasonably straightforward to see how the existence of an ownership relation between Jack and a horse could make it true that Jack *does* own a horse, it is hard to see what sort of thing's existence would necessitate that Jack does *not* own a horse.

We can make the problem more vivid by considering negative existential claims, such as 'There is no horse that is owned by Jack'. On the truthmaker view, all truths require truthmakers, and so even claims about what does not exist have to be made true by things that exist. But what sort of thing's existence would entail that something of a certain kind does *not* exist?

The problem of negative existentials is related to the problem of finding truthmakers for universal claims. Take the claim that all humans are mortal. The mortality of no individual human necessitates that *all* humans are mortal. Moreover, Jack's, Jill's, Hank's, Sara's, and each other person's mortality together don't suffice to necessitate that all humans are mortal, without the additional proviso that those are all the humans there are. But what makes it true that those are all the humans there are? Presumably, it comes down to the fact that there are no other humans, apart from those included in the list, and so we find ourselves once more needing to posit the existence of something that makes it true that something (in this case, more humans) doesn't exist.

Here is a common way for truthmaker theorists to deal with negative and universal claims. They countenance some basic ontology, a catalog of things that suffice to make all affirmative and existential claims true. To this they add a "that's all" fact, which makes it true that there is nothing outside that basic ontology. The "that's all" fact thus provides the needed truthmakers for negative claims and universals. In conjunction with the mortality of each person, it makes true the claim that all humans are mortal. In conjunction with the truthmakers for every claim about what Jack does own, it can make it true that Jack does not own a horse.

Some philosophers are uncomfortable with the idea of a "that's all" fact. For one thing, it seems ad hoc and perhaps even unhelpful. If the problem we face is to explain what makes universal claims true, then positing a universal fact to do so looks like an unhelpful move. What makes it true that "that's all"? The "that's all" fact. And what is the "that's all" fact? It's the thing that makes the claim that that's all there is true.

The truthmaker view is also subject to a complaint that it is really not a theory of truth at all, but rather a principle of metaphysics. Rather than telling us something about the nature of truth, the truthmaker view simply tells us that every true claim has at least one truthmaker. This can be a useful and important insight. It directs us to take seriously the metaphysical implications of our views about what is true or false. Suppose you think it is true that factory farming treats animals cruelly and immorally. The truthmaker view encourages us to ask what exists that makes that true. What makes treating animals in that way cruel and immoral? Answering that question might require positing special moral properties, in addition to the mundane, physical properties of the animals' treatment. Or it might require a detailed theory of the metaphysical grounding of moral truths. Either way, the truthmaker view counsels us to take note of the metaphysical commitments we take on in accepting a claim as true or rejecting it as false.

If someone is interested in our question, 'What is truth?', the truthmaker approach can tell us only that what is true depends on what there is. That might be progress, but it also might be a change of subject. If we want to know what the nature of truth is, we want to know something about *how* the existence of something can necessitate the truth of a claim. Here the truthmaker view has little to say, and a truthmaker theorist is apt to contend that there simply isn't much to say. Necessitation is a brute metaphysical relationship, not the sort of thing whose nature is subject to philosophical exploration. Some contemporary truthmaker theorists, such as David Armstrong, draw their inspiration from early insights of Ludwig Wittgenstein, who would have viewed questions such as "What is the nature of necessitation?" or "What is the nature of truth?" as misuses of language. Any answer to them would be an attempt to say something so fundamental to the operation of language that it is unsayable itself – the linguistic equivalent of trying to see your own eye without using a mirror. "Whereof one cannot speak," Wittgenstein wrote, "one must pass over in silence" (1922, Sect. 7).

In the next chapter, we will see a variation on the theme of not theorizing about the nature of truth. At this point, though, it suffices to remark that truthmaker theories typically emphasize finding truthmakers for various types of claims over explaining the truthmaking relation itself, beyond describing it as a matter of things' existence necessitating claims' truth. Because these views say so little about the nature of the truthmaking relation itself, they are open to the charge of not really explaining the nature of truth at all.

5.6 The Scope Problem

All versions of the correspondence theory face what has come to be known as the Scope Problem. This problem arises because the view appears to be adequate for some sorts of claims, but it also appears to be inadequate for claims of other sorts. A fully satisfactory theory of truth would be fully general. It would tell us the nature of the property that all and only true claims have in common. Ideally, it would do so in a way that also sheds light on what all and only false claims have in common. The correspondence theory of truth, though, seems to fail at characterizing what *all* truths have in common. The Scope Problem arises in different ways for different varieties of the correspondence theory.

Take the classical correspondence view, and consider the claim that Bill Clinton is not an ocelot. The claim is true, and so the view requires that the claim correspond to some obtaining state of affairs. But what state of affairs is it? There seem to be three main options. One is that there are, in addition to such states of affairs as Clinton's being human, being mortal, and being a mammal, further states of affairs consisting in his *not* being an ocelot, *not* being a kangaroo, and *not* being a prime number. Another option is to explain the truth of 'Bill Clinton is not an ocelot' by way of the *non*-obtaining of the state of affairs that Bill Clinton is an ocelot. Both of these moves, though, require embracing some rather strange entities in our ontology – either purely negative states of affairs that obtain (Bill Clinton's not being an ocelot, for example, over and above his being human), or states of affairs that exist without obtaining (Bill Clinton's being an ocelot).

The third possibility would be to take the fact that Bill Clinton is human (a property that precludes his being an ocelot) as what the claim that Bill Clinton is not an ocelot corresponds to. Here we avoid ontological profligacy, but the solution is not satisfactory. Suppose 'Bill Clinton is not an ocelot' corresponds to the state of affairs of Bill Clinton's being human. Of course, 'Bill Clinton is human' also corresponds to that state of affairs. But we might have thought that any two claims that correspond to the same state of affairs would have to be true under precisely the same circumstances; they would have to imply each other. If that is so, 'Bill Clinton is not an ocelot' could not correspond to the same state of affairs as 'Bill Clinton is human', and so it could not correspond to Bill Clinton's being human after all.

The upshot here is that, while the classical correspondence view might seem to do all right at explaining the truth of affirmative claims, such as 'Bill Clinton is human', it appears to be ill suited to deal with negative claims. It also appears to have problems with certain special areas of discourse, such as ethics. Many philosophers think moral properties are something over and above the purely descriptive properties of actions. Suppose that Bev took Mary's wallet, and that it was wrong for her to do that. There is, on this view, no way of analyzing the property of "wrongness" so that it reduces to a complex of purely descriptive properties. There is, in that case, no purely descriptive state of affairs that 'It was wrong for Bev to steal Mary's wallet' corresponds to. Over and above all the purely descriptive facts concerning the theft, we need a further, moral fact, for the claim that it was wrong to correspond to. Again, though, it may be hard to imagine what these purely moral states of affairs are, or what difference their obtaining or not makes to the mind independent world.

The classical correspondence view needs every true claim to correspond to a state of affairs. For some kinds of claims (in particular, negative claims and evaluative claims), that requires positing odd kinds states of affairs that seem to serve no other function than to preserve the correspondence theory. The Scope Problem for classical correspondence arises from its trouble explaining the truth of claims such as 'Bill Clinton is not an ocelot' and 'It was wrong for Bev to steal Mary's wallet'.

The Scope Problem for the causal correspondence theory is similar, and perhaps even more pronounced. The causal correspondence view runs into the problem both in its application of a Tarskian definition of truth in terms of designation and in its application of a causal theory of reference. These features make the theory pretty good at explaining what it means for certain claims to be true, namely claims that refer to ordinary physical objects and properties and whose complexity comes from such logical vocabulary as 'and', 'not', 'or', and 'something'. But it has trouble accounting for the truth of claims about abstract objects such as numbers and of claims concerning mathematical or moral properties, because the causal theory of reference has trouble explaining how terms could designate such things. The theory also has trouble accounting for the truth of complex claims concerning what might have happened but did not, and for complex claims involving terms such as 'because', since the Tarskian way of defining truth in terms of designation falters on those claims. Thus it seems the causal correspondence theory is unable to give a fully general account of truth, good for true claims of all sorts.

The truthmaker version of the correspondence theory of truth can be applied to claims of almost any kind. However, it still has difficulties with universal claims and negative claims, which require it, ultimately, to posit a "that's all" fact to make them true. Again, though, the "that's all" fact can seem to be a purely ad hoc posit, whose only motivation is that the truthmaker view requires it. The truthmaker view's version of the Scope Problem, then, is that it does a more satisfactory job of explaining the truth of affirmative, non-universal claims than it does of accounting for negative or universal claims. It seems not to work well as a theory of truth in general.

Correspondence theorists have three main options available to them in response to the Scope Problem. One (which works better for classical correspondence and the truthmaker views), is to bite the bullet and posit whatever sorts of things are needed for the difficult claims to come out true. Negative states of affairs, evaluative states of affairs, existing but non-obtaining states of affairs, and the "that's all" fact might all seem strange, but a correspondence theorist could point out that mere strangeness is an insufficient reason to dismiss such entities out of hand, especially since positing them appears necessary for a correspondence theory of truth to work.

The second and third options, which work better for causal correspondence views than for classical or truthmaker views, involve rejecting realism about the problematic claims. One might instead adopt an anti-realist view, according to which the truth of the problematic claims depends on what people believe or can know. Although such anti-realism might be implausible for claims such as 'Jack has never ridden an emu', which cause difficulties for the classical and the truthmaker accounts, it is much more attractive for mathematical claims, for claims about morality, for modal claims (claims concerning necessity and possibility), and for explanatory claims using terms such as 'because'. To make this view work, the correspondence theorist would have to explain how people's beliefs (or their abilities to know things) provide what the correspondence theory needs. So, for example, an advocate of causal correspondence would have to treat 'wrong' as designating, not a property of actions in themselves, but a relational property actions have in virtue of the ways people are disposed to judge them.

The third option is simply to deny that the problematic claims have truth values; they are neither true nor false. This might not help classical and truthmaker views, though, as it would deprive claims such as 'Bill Clinton is not an ocelot' of truth values. But it might work for causal correspondence views, requiring only that we think of claims about abstract objects and properties, evaluative claims, and explanatory or modal claims as, strictly speaking, neither true nor false.

In any case, these moves face the same objections. Claims such as 'Eleven is a prime number', 'It is usually wrong to steal food from hungry people', and 'Bill Clinton is not an ocelot' seem literally and mind-independently true. Preserving that intuition requires a theory of truth compatible with realism about mathematical truth, moral truth, and the truth of negative claims. These non-realist responses to the Scope Problem thus save correspondence theories of truth, but they do so at the cost of realism, and that cost might be too much to pay.

5.7 The Equivalence Principle, Realism, and the Value of Truth

To evaluate a theory of truth properly, we must consider how it fares with respect to the Equivalence Principle, realism, and the value of truth. Let us look at correspondence theories with respect to each of these in turn.

At first blush, correspondence theories appear to do well with respect to the Equivalence Principle. This is because 'corresponds to the facts' is an expression we sometimes use as just a wordier synonym for 'is true'. Thus, we might expect that the instances of 'The claim that _ corresponds to the facts if, and only if, _' to hold, since it is means the same 'It is true that _ if, and only if, _'. Nevertheless, when we work out the details of what correspondence is and what it means for a claim to correspond to the facts, things become much less clear.

The classical correspondence view, which posits a state of affairs for every claim to assert to obtain, does fine here. States of affairs that obtain are facts, and true claims correspond to facts by asserting, of obtaining states of affairs, that they obtain. So long as we are willing to posit all the facts the theory requires, including negative facts, moral facts, mathematical facts, and modal facts, it will turn out that all and only true claims correspond to facts and the Equivalence Principle will be satisfied. But if we balk at positing all the required facts, there will be some non-paradoxical T-biconditionals that are not true.

The causal correspondence view likewise does well with the Equivalence Principle, but not perfectly. The idea that we should require a theory of truth to deliver the T-biconditionals is actually due to Tarski, and one of his most important contributions was to show that the definition of truth in terms of designation actually *implies* the T-biconditionals, for all the claims the definition applies to. The causal correspondence theory's variety of the Scope Problem, though, also points to difficulties it can have with the Equivalence Principle. Take the claim 'The glass broke because Jack hit it with a hammer'. This is the sort of claim for which a definition of truth in terms of designation runs into difficulties. While the following may be *consistent* with the causal correspondence theory of truth:

(13) It is true that the glass broke because Jack hit it with a hammer if, and only if, the glass broke because Jack hit it with a hammer.

the definition of truth in terms of designation does not imply it. To see why, suppose we have settled what 'glass', 'broke', 'Jack', 'hit', and 'hammer' designate, so that we have determined the truth values of 'The glass broke' and 'Jack hit the glass with a hammer'. That is still not enough to tell us whether the glass broke *because* Jack hit it with a hammer. We cannot give truth conditions for claims of the form 'A because B' simply in terms of the truth conditions of A and B.

A fully adequate theory of truth, though, should not only be consistent with the T-biconditionals; it should imply them. Similar problems arise for claims about abstract objects and properties, for which the causal theory of reference fails.

It is the truthmaker view, though, that runs into the most severe problems with the Equivalence Principle. The view is consistent with the T-biconditionals, but it does nothing to explain why they hold, and there is nothing in the view itself that entails them. According to the truthmaker view, for a claim to be true is for something to exist whose existence necessitates the truth of the claim. To give us the T-biconditionals, though, more is needed.

Consider the claim that Eve owns an apple. According to the truthmaker view, the claim that Eve owns an apple is true if, and only if, something exists whose existence necessitates that the claim is true. By itself, that is not enough to give us:

(14) The claim that Eve owns an apple is true if, and only if, Eve owns an apple.

This is because the following, all by itself:

(15) Something exists whose existence necessitates that the claim that Eve owns an apple is true.

does not imply this:

(16) Eve owns an apple.

Nor does 'Eve owns an apple', all by itself, imply 'Something exists whose existence necessitates that the claim that Eve owns an apple is true'. To get these additional implications, which are needed for the truthmaker view to imply the T-biconditionals, we need some further assumptions. In this case, we need to assume:

(17) If the claim that Eve owns an apple is true, then Eve owns an apple.

as well as:

(18) If Eve owns an apple, then the claim that Eve owns an apple is true.

Here, then, is the problem. We can't infer the T-biconditionals from the truthmaker theory itself, unless we add assumptions like (17) and (18). Adding those assumptions, though, amount to adding the T-biconditionals themselves. Taken together, (17) and (18) just say 'The claim that Eve own an apple is true if, and only if, Eve owns an apple'. This shows that, even though the truthmaker view is compatible with the instances of the Equivalence Schema, it does not do anything to explain them, and they do not fall out as logical consequences of the theory.

One could try to avoid this problem by modifying the truthmaker view somewhat. Rather than saying that a truthmaker for a claim is something whose existence necessitates that the claim is true, a truthmaker theorist could say that a truthmaker for a claim is something that necessitates the *claim itself*. For example, a truthmaker for 'Eve owns an apple' would be anything that necessitates that Eve owns an apple, rather than anything that necessitates that the claim that Eve owns an apple is true. However, one might justifiably ask at that point where truth has gone in the truthmaker version of the correspondence view. We would still need an explanation of how something's necessitating that Eve owns an apple suffices to explain the truth of the claim that Eve owns an apple. After all, Eve's property of owning an apple is very different from the claim's property of being true. To link Eve's apple ownership to the claim's truth, we are apparently going to have to appeal to something like the Equivalence Principle itself, and so the original problem remains.

Correspondence theories fare better with realism than with Equivalence Principle. Realist intuitions are the main motivator for correspondence theories of truth. According to realism, some claims are true mind-independently, which is to say, regardless of what anyone ever believes or could know. Correspondence theories make room for claims to be true or false in virtue of how things are in the mind-independent world. The truth of the claim that electrons are negatively charged, for example, is a matter of its relationship to the charge of electrons, not its relationship to what we think or to what we could know. Especially with respect to scientific claims or claims about physical objects and properties, the correspondence theory promises to explain the nature of truth in terms of relationships between claims and their subject matter, rather than relationships between claims and us who believe, assert, or attempt to know them.

Nevertheless, we have seen that versions of the correspondence theory can and sometimes do fail to deliver on their realist promise. Evaluative claims, modal claims, explanatory claims, mathematical claims, and even negative and universal claims all supply hard cases for the versions of the correspondence theory examined in this chapter. Advocates of the correspondence theory can take the anti-realist option with respect to these claims, but this limits the reach of their realism. The correspondence theory is consistent with some claims' being true mind-independently, but maybe not as many as we initially thought.

It is worth pointing out that the correspondence theory is also compatible with most forms of anti-realism. One need only take the view that what true claims correspond to are, in some sense, mental entities or things whose existence depends on our ways of thinking about them. If the obtaining of a state of affairs depends on what people believe, then an anti-realist version of the classical correspondence view could be readily formulated. If our terms designate objects that are partly constituted by what we think or what we could know, then an anti-realist version of the causal correspondence view is possible. Likewise, an anti-realist truthmaker view is possible, on which mental states are the truthmakers for all true claims.

We saw in the previous chapter that epistemic theories of truth are not compatible with realism. Correspondence theories are compatible with both anti-realism and realism. This could be to their credit. It means that we can take questions about the mind-independence of different types of claims one-by-one. Rather than having a theory of truth that dictates from the start that truth is always (or never) mind-dependent, we can let the theory of truth remain in the background and take on particular questions directly, such as the question whether it is objectively true that torturing babies for fun is wrong. But, as we have also seen in this chapter, things might not work out so easily in practice. A causal correspondence theory, for example, might require us to adopt an anti-realist view of morality.

Finally, let us consider how well correspondence theories explain the value of truth. Here they appear to do especially badly. Suppose truth is correspondence, in the sense of one of the theories discussed in this chapter. Still we might wonder why we should care whether our beliefs correspond to reality in that sense. Why should beliefs that correspond be better – intrinsically, instrumentally, or telically – than beliefs that do not? While epistemic theories tie the notion of truth quite directly to the notion of goodness – recall James's remark that the true is the good in the way of belief – the connection between truth and value is much looser on a correspondence view.

A correspondence theorist could attempt to give *some* explanation for the value of truth. Even though there is nothing obviously intrinsically valuable about the correspondence relation, there is still plenty of room for correspondence theorists to adopt some further explanation of truth's value as the aim of belief or as instrumentally or telically valuable. Ordinarily, such further explanations will concern the nature of belief, action, or assertion, rather than the nature of truth. That is, the value of truth would stem from the role it plays in guiding belief, or action, or assertion, rather than from its nature directly. Those who expect a theory of truth's nature also to provide an explanation of its value might be disappointed by that result, but correspondence theorists can reply that the fault lies in the expectation. Truth's value, they can say, is outside its nature.

Although correspondence theories may improve on epistemic theories in many ways, they still face serious problems. The twentieth century saw the rise of some new kinds of theory of truth. The most popular alternative is "deflationism," and it is the topic of the following chapter.

Further Reading

Varieties of what we're calling "classical" correspondence views are defended by Wittgenstein (1922), and Russell (1906; 1912). Armstrong (1997) elaborates the metaphysics of states of affairs, and his (2004) develops a theory of truthmaking. Rodriguez-Pereyra (2006) provides a good discussion of truthmaking.

Tarski (1944) sets out his approach to defining truth in terms of designation, and Field (1972) extends the approach to develop a causal correspondence theory. Interested readers should consult those articles for a much more technical presentation of the Tarskian strategy for defining truth, which is in many ways superior to its summary in this chapter.

Philip Kitcher (2002) defends the view that the causal correspondence theory of truth is needed to explain the connection between true believing and successful action, and Wrenn (2011) argues against Kitcher's approach.

An unorthodox approach to the correspondence theory is the theory of truth as "indirect correspondence," a view defended by Terence Horgan (Horgan & Potrč 2000; Horgan 2001).

For more on many of the topics covered in this chapter, see the *Stanford Encyclopedia of Philosophy* entries, "The Correspondence Theory of Truth" (David 2013), "Facts" (Mulligan & Correia 2013), "Truthmakers" (MacBride 2013), "States of Affairs" (Textor 2012) and their bibliographies.

6
Deflationary Theories of Truth

6.1 A New Way to Think About Truth

Epistemic theories of truth start from the idea that truth is what our tests for truth test for. They run into problems because they give mind independent reality too small a role in determining what is true. Correspondence theories start from the idea that truth is a matter of corresponding to how the world is. They appear not to be able to account for the truth of some kinds of claims, and they may face skeptical problems as well.

In the twentieth century, some new ways of thinking about truth emerged, aimed at avoiding the problems of epistemic theories and correspondence theories as well. The most influential family of theories, *deflationist* theories of truth, drew inspiration from developments in formal logic. Deflationary theories typically start from the idea that calling a claim true is very little different from simply asserting the claim itself. I could tell you that snow is white, or I could say pretty much the same thing in more words, by saying, "It is true that snow is white." What if that equivalence is all there is to understand about truth?

Philosophers often aim to describe the essential natures of properties. In giving a theory of justice, for example, they aim to explain what makes a states of affairs just (or unjust), and what all and only just states of affairs have in common. Deflationists reject that approach when it comes to truth. There need not be anything that all and only true claims have in common, in virtue of which they are true. Rather, they think, the logical behavior of expressions such as '_ is true' tells us all there is to know about the nature of truth, such as it is. Understanding truth is understanding the logical relationship between 'It is true that _' and whatever claim fills the blank.

There are many varieties of deflationism, differing from one another in the details of how they explain the logical function of expressions such as '_ is true'. This chapter will survey three influential versions of deflationism: Frank Ramsey's redundancy theory, W. V. Quine's disquotational theory, and Paul Horwich's minimalist theory.

6.2 The Redundancy Theory

One of the earliest statements of a deflationary view of truth is due to Frank Ramsey (1927). He considered two sorts of cases, which we will call "direct" and "indirect" truth attributions. In a direct truth attribution, one explicitly spells out a claim and says that it is true. Each of the following would then be a direct truth attribution: 'It is true that snow is white', 'The claim that Caesar was murdered is true', 'It's a fact that ocelots are carnivorous'. In contrast, indirect truth attributions do not spell out explicitly the content of a claim. They instead identify claims in some other way, and say that those claims are true. Some examples of indirect truth attributions are the following: 'Jack Sprat's latest claim about the nutritional value of fat is true', 'What Brutus said to you yesterday was true', 'All the theorems of Peano Arithmetic are true'.

In the case of direct truth attributions, Ramsey thought of the expression 'is true' (and its variations) as strictly redundant. 'It is true that Caesar was murdered' means exactly the same thing as 'Caesar was murdered'. If we use the wordier formulation, it can only be for reasons of style or emphasis, since there is no difference in meaning between the two.

Ramsey's view is bolder than the trivial observation that Caesar was murdered if, and only if, it is true that Caesar was murdered. Ramsey thought the relationship between 'Caesar was murdered' and 'It is true that Caesar was murdered' is on par with the relationship between 'Someone stole the money' and 'The money was stolen by someone.' It is a relationship of strict synonymy; they have exactly the same meaning.

To see how bold this claim really is, notice the apparent difference between 'Caesar was murdered' and 'The claim that Caesar was murdered is true'. The first sentence says that a *person* (Caesar) has the property of having been murdered. Going by its surface structure, the second sentence is quite different. It says that a *claim* (viz., the claim that Caesar was murdered) has the property of being true. The first sentence does not say anything about claims or truth, and the second mentions Caesar and murder only obliquely. Their surface structures suggest that these two sentences have quite different contents.

In proposing that the expression 'is true' is redundant, then, Ramsey is proposing that the surface structures in these cases are misleading. 'It is true that Caesar was murdered' turns out not to attribute the property of truth to anything. It's just a wordier way of attributing the property of having been murdered to Caesar.

We would not need expressions such as 'is true' (which are called "truth predicates") if all truth attributions were direct. The truth predicate proves necessary when, for whatever reason, we are unable to state explicitly the claim or claims we are calling true. In *indirect* truth attributions, then, we say things such as 'What he told you was true' or 'All the theorems of Peano Arithmetic are true.' Ramsey thinks we can account for these uses of the truth predicate, though, without having to suppose such claims are in the business of attributing a property to claims.

On Ramsey's view, indirect truth attributions express infinite conjunctions of claims. 'What he told you was true' is just a way of expressing the infinite conjunction of all the instances of 'If he told you that _, then it's true that _', where the two blanks are to be filled in by the same sentence:

(1)   If he told you that water is nutritious, then it is true that water is nutritious, AND
if he told you that the sky is blue, then it is true that the sky is blue, AND
if he told you that Peterson embezzled the money, then it is true that Peterson embezzled the money, AND ...

Look at the right hand side of all these sentences. Each of them is a *direct* truth attribution, which, on Ramsey's view, means that the 'it is true that' expression is redundant. 'What he told you was true' thus turns out to mean the same as an infinitely long conjunction that includes clauses such as:

(2)   If he told you that water is nutritious, then water is nutritious, AND
if he told you that the sky is blue, then the sky is blue, AND
if he told you that Peterson embezzled the money, then Peterson embezzled the money, AND ...

One of the most philosophically important aspects of Ramsey's approach is that it seems to account for our use of the truth predicate without ever treating '_ is true' as attributing a property to a thing. If the proposal works, then it shows how we can account for the logic and usage of the truth predicate without actually having to suppose that there is any such property as truth! 'It is true that' and its variations become a piece of ordinary logical vocabulary, much like 'something', 'nothing', and 'and'.

If all that is correct, then there is no problem of understanding the nature of truth. Once Caesar's murder is fully explained, there is nothing else to explain about the truth of the claim that Caesar was murdered, for "the truth of the claim that Caesar was murdered" is nothing over and above Caesar's having been murdered.

There are powerful reasons for thinking the redundancy view cannot work for indirect truth attributions, though.

One involves doubts about whether the idea of an inf
conjunction of claims really makes any sense at all. We
familiar with claims that have only finitely many components,
and we are familiar with conjunctions that are only finitely
long. The redundancy theory contends that indirect truth
attributions are *infinitely long* conjunctions, but no one has
ever uttered or understood such a conjunction. How, then,
could it be possible for us to understand indirect truth
attributions?

Another problem for the redundancy theory also has to do
with our ability to understand indirect truth attributions.
Consider this claim:

(3)   The third sentence on page 42 of Jones's *Ichthyology* is
      true.

Intuitively, it seems that I can understand (3) perfectly well
without ever knowing what the third sentence on page 42 of
Jones's *Ichthyology* is. But imagine that the sentence in question is:

(4)   Some pelagic fish are ovoviviparous.

That is a sentence I do not understand, and that is
where the problem comes from. According to the redundancy
theory, (3) expresses an infinite conjunction of claims of
the form:

(5)   If the third sentence on page 42 of Jones's *Ichthyology*
      says that _, then _.

The crucial conjunct in that infinite conjunction is this one:

(6)   If the third sentence on page 42 of Jones's *Ichthyology*
      says that some pelagic fish are ovoviviparous, then some
      pelagic fish are ovoviviparous.

Since I can't understand (4), I can't understand (6) either.
But (6) is the most important conjunct in the infinite conjunction that (3) expresses – it is the only one whose antecedent

holds. Given the redundancy theory, then, it would appear that I cannot understand (3) without understanding (6). And, because I can't understand (6), it would then follow that I cannot understand (3) after all! The redundancy theory has a problem explaining how someone could understand an indirect truth attribution without understanding the claim it says is true.

This problem extends to direct truth attributions as well. I can understand 'The claim that some pelagic fish are ovoviviparous is true' without being able to understand 'Some pelagic fish are ovoviviparous'. If the truth predicate were redundant, I could not understand the truth attribution without being able to understand the claim it attributes truth to.

A related problem arises from considerations about evidence. Consider the sorts of things that might be evidence for (3). Some of that evidence might include the facts that Jones herself is a highly regarded and careful ichthyologist who rarely makes mistakes, that the book was carefully vetted and reviewed by an independent panel of experts, that the publisher has issued errata for the book that include no corrections to page 42, and so on. We could gather a great deal of evidence that the sentence on page 42 is true *without* having to know what the sentence says or having to bring to bear any ichthyological data. On the other hand, none of those things seem to be evidence that some pelagic fish are ovoviviparous. To find out whether any pelagic fish are ovoviviparous, we need to know about fish, not about the publication history of a book about fish. On the redundancy theory, though, (3) either boils down to 'Some pelagic fish are ovoviviparous' or it expresses an infinite conjunction of instances of (5). In the former case, we would be committed to treating evidence about the publication history of Jones's *Ichthyology* as evidence that bears on whether there are pelagic fish, and that might seem wrong. In the latter case, we are not much better off. The publication of the history of the book might not be evidence that some pelagic fish are ovoviviparous, but would turn out to be evidence that *either* some pelagic fish are ovoviviparous *or* the third sentence on page 42 of Jones's *Ichthyology* doesn't say they are, and that might seem no less counterintuitive.

The redundancy theory also faces a problem involving explanation. Especially if we have realist inclinations, it is natural to suppose:

(7) 'Water is a liquid at room temperature' is true because water is a liquid at room temperature.

However, on the redundancy theory, (7) means the same as:

(8) Water is a liquid at room temperature because water is a liquid at room temperature.

The trouble is that (7) seems to be a correct explanation, but (8) seems false or, at best, circular and uninformative. If they mean the same thing, though, then (7) couldn't be true or informative while (8) is not. If we accept the redundancy theory, we seem forced to conclude either that (7) is as unacceptable as (8), or that (8) is just as acceptable as (7). Neither option is attractive.

6.3 Disquotationalism

A close cousin of the redundancy theory is *disquotationalism*. Its most prominent defenders have been W. V. Quine and Hartry Field. Like Ramsey, Quine held that the truth predicate serves a purely logical function. In cases of direct truth attributions, that function is "disquotation" or "semantic descent."

Disquotationalists think of sentences as the primary truth bearers. For various reasons, we sometimes find ourselves talking about sentences, and to do that we need ways to give sentences names. One way is to use quotation marks. So

(9) Water is a liquid at room temperature.

says something about water, while

(10) 'Water is a liquid at room temperature' has seven words.

and

(11) 'Water is a liquid at room temperature' is grammatical
      in English.

are not about water at all. They are both about the sentence,
'Water is a liquid at room temperature'. The effect of the
quotation marks is to create a name for a sentence.

As Quine puts it, the truth predicate cancels out the effect
of quotation marks. If we say:

(12) 'Water is a liquid at room temperature' is true.

our use of 'is true' undoes the work the quotation marks
originally did. It lets us descend from talk about sentences to
talk once more about the world. Quine says, "... the truth
predicate serves, as it were, to point through the sentence to
the reality; it serves as a reminder that though sentences are
mentioned, reality is still the whole point" (1970, p. 11).

So far, this all very similar to the redundancy theory, but
there is a subtle difference. A redundancy theorist would say
that "Water is liquid at room temperature' is true' *means the
same thing* as 'Water is liquid at room temperature'. A disquotationalist such as Quine, on the other hand, can remain
silent on the matter of meaning and be content to point out
that, whatever the relationship between their meanings,
"Water is liquid at room temperature' is true' is logically
equivalent (given the meaning of 'Water is liquid at room
temperature') to 'Water is liquid at room temperature'.

To get a sense of this difference, consider an imaginary
debate among three people, Alice, Bob, and Carol, over the
relationship between

(13) The bottle is empty.

and

(14) It's not the case that the bottle is not empty.

Alice thinks the two sentences mean different things. While
(13) asserts that the bottle is empty, she says, (14) denies that

the bottle isn't empty. Bob disagrees. According to Bo͐
sentence and its double negation always mean exactly ιℎℯ
same thing. So, on his view, (13) means the same thing as
(14). Finally, Carol contends that the question whether (13)
and (14) mean the same thing is idle, since everyone agrees
that a sentence and its double negation are logically equivalent to one another – each entails the other.

A redundancy theorist such as Ramsey takes a position
analogous to Bob's. Ramsey thinks 'Water is a liquid at room
temperature' and 'It is true that water is a liquid at room
temperature' mean the same thing. A disquotationalist such
as Quine might think the question of whether the sentences
mean the same thing is idle, at least in this context. Once we
see that each entails the other (given the meaning of 'Water
is liquid at room temperature'), we have seen all that matters
about their relationship.

This difference matters to how the two types of deflationism handle indirect truth attributions. A disquotationalist can
avoid some problems these attributions cause for the redundancy theory. Consider (3) above, 'The third sentence on page
42 of Jones's *Ichthyology* is true'. A redundancy theorist will
treat this as expressing an infinite conjunction of instances of
(5). A disquotationalist can take a different tack. For the
disquotationalist, what matters about (3) is that it is meant
to be logically interchangeable with the third sentence on
page 42 of Jones's *Ichthyology*. Given what sentence that is,
it and (3) entail one another. Likewise, 'All the theorems of
Peano Arithmetic are true' entails, and is entailed by, all the
theorems of Peano Arithmetic (given a background assumption to the effect that those are all the theorems of Peano
Arithmetic). This sort of logical equivalence is not the same
as sameness of meaning, but a disquotationalist need not
make any claims about sameness of meaning at all.

Quine emphasizes that the truth predicate provides a
mechanism for saying things that, due to our limited resources,
we would be unable to say otherwise. There are infinitely
many theorems of Peano Arithmetic, for example, and we are
not able to assert them all one by one. Nevertheless, we can
generalize over all of them and say that all the theorems of
Peano Arithmetic are thus-and-so. The truth predicate allows
us to generalize over the *sentences* that are theorems of Peano

arithmetic, and then to disquote them in one stroke, thereby saying something about numbers that we could not say except by first talking about sentences about numbers.

Like the redundancy theory, disquotationalism takes very seriously the idea that the truth predicate is a piece of logical vocabulary, functioning more like 'all', 'and', or 'not' than like predicates such as 'is green'. There is no such thing as "the nature of conjunction" or "the nature of universal generalization" for us to understand, over and above the logic of conjunctions and universal generalizations. For the disquotationalist, there is also no such thing as "the nature of truth" for us to understand, over and above our understanding of the logic of the truth predicate. Furthermore, the disquotationalist believes, the logic of the truth predicate is the logic of disquotation. Once we say that '_ is true' is logically equivalent to whatever sentence fills the '_', and that 'Every sentence that is such-and-such is true' entails, and is entailed by, every sentence that is such-and-such (given, as always, the background assumption that those are the such-and-such sentences), we have understood all there is to understand about truth.

Disquotationalism does not solve all the redundancy theory's problems, though. First, Hartry Field has argued that disquotationalists must accept that they do not really understand the meaning of truth attributions to sentences they do not understand. For example, consider 'Franz's testimony to the commission was true', and suppose that Franz's testimony was entirely in German, a language I do not know. On the disquotationalist view, understanding 'Franz's testimony to the commission was true' is a matter of appreciating that it entails Franz's testimony and is entailed by that testimony (given the background assumption that that is Franz's testimony). Since I don't understand Franz's testimony, though, I am in no position to appreciate that it entails or is entailed by anything. So, my understanding of 'Franz's testimony to the commission was true' is at best imperfect.

Some disquotationalists are apt to think that this is not a very serious problem. Recall that the point of having a truth predicate is to allow us to say things that we otherwise could not say. Usually, disquotationalists point out that the truth predicate lets us assert claims or collections of claims that we, in our finitude, could not assert. However, they might also point to another useful function of the truth predicate: It allows us to assert (or at least agree with) claims that we do not understand.

Another possible disquotationalist response is to appeal to translation. When I say, 'Snow is white', I have said something logically equivalent to a German sentence I do not understand. That is no cause for alarm, though, because we think of the English and German sentences as intertranslatable. Who cares that I don't understand a German sentence, if I understand its English translation? A disquotationalist might say the situation is the same with indirect truth attributions. If I say (in English) 'Franz's testimony to the commission was true', I have said something logically equivalent to the English translation of Franz's testimony, and my ability to understand that translation (and to understand that it is a translation of Franz's testimony) suffices for me to be able to understand the truth attribution.

The appeal to translations immediately runs into the problem of the so-called "indeterminacy of translation." This is the view (which is controversial) that unless we make an appeal to propositions as primary truth bearers and as the meanings of sentences, there will inevitably be more than one way of translating the sentences of one language into another, and the resulting translations will not be logically equivalent to one another. Given the indeterminacy of translation, which is something both Quine and Field accept, it would then turn out to be *indeterminate* what I have said when I say that Franz's testimony was true. That is, there would be no fact of the matter as to what I have said or as to whether my claim is true! One might try to avoid this problem by picking out some way of translating German to English as the "canonical" translation, so that my claim is equivalent to the canonical translation of Franz's testimony.

The appeal to a canonical translation, though, brings its own problems. First, given the indeterminacy of translation, the only thing that makes a translation canonical is the fact that we accept it as canonical. This invites a kind of relativism about truth. Whether or not Franz's testimony was true depends on what we take its canonical translation to be. That makes truth depend on us in a way that people with realist inclinations are apt to find unacceptable. Second, because I do not speak German, I have no idea what the canonical way of translating German into English is. Having no idea how to translate Franz's testimony into English, we are back in the situation of my not knowing what I have said when I say that Franz's testimony was true.

Another problem, independent of the indeterminacy of translation, is the disquotationalist appeal to translation might get the cart before the horse. Intuitively, what makes a translation correct has something to do with truth: A good translation of Franz's testimony must be true under exactly the same circumstances as Franz's original testimony, and we can criticize a translation as bad, or as not preserving Franz's meaning, if its truth conditions are different from those of what Franz actually said. None of those intuitions would make sense, though, unless we could apply our concept of truth directly to Franz's testimony, rather than only indirectly by way of a canonical translation. If the notion of good translation depends on our understanding that foreign utterances can be true, we can't explain how the truth predicate applies to foreign utterances by appeal to translation.

Disquotationalists thus have several options, each of which is unattractive in some way or other. They could give up the powerful intuition that I can understand 'Franz's testimony to the commission was true' without understanding German. They could maintain that there is no fact of the matter as to the truth value of 'Franz's testimony to the commission was true'. They could relativize truth to languages and translation schemes, so that there can be a determinate truth value for sentences of the form 'The translation of Franz's testimony into my language according to system S is true', while allowing that the sentence is true for some values of S and not for others. Or, they could avoid the problem of the indeterminacy of translation by positing propositions as the primary truth bearers and the meanings of sentences.

This last option might seem to be best, but it comes at a high price for disquotationalists. Disquotationalists see the truth predicate as a logical device for talking about the world by way of talking about sentences. If propositions are the primary truth-bearers, then it would seem that disquotationalism has missed the point of a theory of truth. We immediately face the question of what it is for a *proposition* to be true. A theory of how the truth predicate operates with respect to sentences tells us nothing about that at all.

The explanatory problem for the redundancy theory also haunts disquotationalism. According to disquotationalism:

(15) 'Water is liquid at room temperature' is true because water is liquid at room temperature.

is logically equivalent to

(16) Water is liquid at room temperature because water is liquid at room temperature.

Nevertheless, it appears that (15) is true and (16) is not, which is inconsistent with disquotationalism.

The best disquotationalist responses to this problem are either to deny that (15) is true or to deny that (15) and (16) are logically equivalent. How could (15) be false? A disquotationalist could say (15) only seems to be true because we mistakenly suppose that the truth predicate is not a purely logical device. On the contrary, (15) does not attribute the property of truth to 'Water is liquid at room temperature' any more than 'There is nothing in the box' attributes a location to some nothing. Once we see that 'is true' is a purely logical device, we will see that (15) is false. 'Water is liquid at room temperature' isn't true because water is liquid at room temperature. Rather, the explanation of its truth is the same as the explanation of water's liquidity at room temperature.

The other alternative is to deny that the claims are equivalent. When we assert (15), we are saying imprecisely what we would say more precisely in the following way:

(17) 'Water is liquid at room temperature' is true because (a) 'Water is liquid at room temperature' means that water is liquid at room temperature and (b) water is liquid at room temperature.

That claim, however, is obviously not equivalent to (16).

If we see part of the content of (15) as involving a claim about what 'Water is liquid at room temperature' means, then we need not take it to be equivalent to the false explanation of why water is liquid at room temperature.

6.4   Minimalism

Paul Horwich (1998) has defended a third version of deflationism, which he calls *minimalism*. This view differs from disquotationalism in a couple of important ways. First, minimalism takes the primary truth bearers to be propositions rather than sentences. Second, minimalism is compatible with the view that truth is a property of some sort; it does not treat the truth predicate as a purely logical device.

Although minimalism is *compatible* with the view that truth is a property, it is not committed to that view. Minimalism involves three key claims:

(18)   Truth is a logical property at most; in particular, it is not a substantive property whose nature is explained by a philosophical theory.

(19)   Once we understand the rules that govern the *concept of truth*, we will have understood everything there is to understand about the nature of truth.

(20)   The concept of truth is the concept whose applications are governed by an *a priori* commitment to the non-paradoxical instances of: 'The proposition that p is true if, and only if, p'. The collection of these instances is all the theory of truth we could possibly need.

Let us consider these claims one by one. The first claim, that truth is a logical property at most, is what makes minimalism a variety of deflationism. A "substantive property" is a property with an underlying nature. The underlying nature of the property explains how things that have it are related to other things. Consider, for example, the property of being at a temperature of 30°C. The nature of temperature has to do with the average kinetic energy of the molecules that constitute something. When something is 30°C, it has that temperature in virtue of the kinetic energy of its molecules. Moreover, we can explain why things that are 30°C behave as they do in terms of that energy. For example, we can use the kinetic energy of the molecules to explain why a certain amount of a gas exerts a certain amount of pressure when it is 30°C. Temperature is a substantive property.

Truth, on the minimalist (and, really, on any deflationist) view, is not a property like that. The error of correspondence and epistemic theories is to try to find some underlying nature of truth, which will explain something about the relationship of true claims to the rest of the world. According to minimalism, there is no such underlying nature to find. Instead, the predicate "is true" exists to serve the same sorts of logical functions disquotationalists and redundancy theorists say it serves. It allows us to make indirect truth attributions, which enables us to say things we could not say otherwise, such as 'All the theorems of Peano Arithmetic are true' or 'Whatever your grandmother told you about saving money was true'.

If truth is not a substantive property, and if the truth predicate plays a purely logical role, then that means truth is a merely logical property or no property at all. Disquotationalism and the redundancy theory are committed to truth's being no property at all. Minimalists could agree with them about that, but they do not have to. On the minimalist view, the truth predicate could be a genuinely descriptive predicate, rather than just a logical operator. What's important to minimalism is that there is nothing that all and only true propositions have in common in virtue of which they are true, and the minimalist need not take a position on whether or not that means truth is not a property.

The second claim of minimalism is closely related to the first, and it is similar to claims made by other forms of deflationism. To understand truth, on the minimalist view, we need to understand how the *concept* of truth works, and in particular what rules govern our applications of the concept to propositions. This is similar to the redundancy and disquotationalist ideas that all there is to understanding truth is an understanding of the logical role of the truth predicate.

This makes understanding truth rather different from understanding some other philosophically important properties, such as moral rightness, for example. On the most popular meta-ethical views, a philosophical theory of moral rightness needs to tell us what features of actions make them right or wrong. Thus consequentialist theories claim that what makes an action right or wrong has to do with the goodness or badness of its consequences, and deontological theories claim that what makes actions right or wrong has to do with whether it fulfills or violates a duty.

Compare this to the logical concept of *conjunction*. To understand this concept is to understand two matters of logic: (i) that the conjunction of any two claims, A and B, follows from those two claims together, and (ii) that each of the claims, A and B, follows from their conjunction. Once one understands that, one understands all there is to understand about conjunction.

The third component of minimalism is a specific view about what rules govern the concept of truth. Here minimalism gives a central role to a version of the Equivalence Schema. According to minimalism, the truth concept is governed by our disposition to accept all the non-paradoxical instances of this schema:

(21)   <P> is true if, and only if, P.

where '<P>' is a blank to be filled in with a name for a proposition, and 'P' is a blank to be filled in with a sentence that expresses that proposition. We will refer to (21) as the *Propositional Equivalence Schema* or PES. Horwich calls the collection of the schema's non-paradoxical instances the *minimal theory of truth*, and *minimalism* is the view that the minimal theory of truth is all the theory of truth we can hope for.

Like redundancy theorists and disquotationalists, minimalists think the point of the concept of truth is to enable us to express or think with claims we otherwise could not. Take the claim, 'All the theorems of Peano Arithmetic are true'. (Peano Arithmetic is a set of axioms for basic arithmetic.) We need the truth predicate to express that claim, since there are infinitely many theorems of Peano Arithmetic. Together with the PES, the claim implies every instance of:

(22)   If <P> is a theorem of Peano Arithmetic, then P.

Without a truth predicate, we could not assert a claim that implies precisely the instances of (22), but the truth predicate makes such an assertion possible.

(It is important to bear in mind that (22) is a *schema*, not a sentence. The 'P's are just labels for blanks that are to be filled in with the same sentence in each case. We could just as easily have written it as 'If it is a theorem of Peano Arithmetic that _, then _', which doesn't look like a sentence at all.)

In his book *Truth*, Horwich goes to great lengths to try to show how a concept governed by the PES could do all the work we want from the concept of truth, without requiring us to suppose there is something all and only true propositions have in common in virtue of which they are true.

Minimalism avoids some of the redundancy theory and disquotationalism's problems. Instead of appealing to infinitely long conjunctions, which can be problematic, minimalism relies on our acceptance of the instances of the T-schema to explain how indirect truth attributions can work. Minimalism also need not restrict the truth predicate to sentences one understands. This is because minimalism is framed in terms of propositions, rather than sentences. Consider the case of Franz's testimony to the commission. If I say, 'Franz's testimony to the commission was true', the Equivalence Schema and my assertion imply all the instances of:

(23)   If Franz testified to the commission that _, then _.

It does not matter that I don't understand Franz's German utterances. What matters is that I have said something that implies all the propositions Franz asserted, regardless of what language he asserted them in.

This flexibility also gives me a way to assert propositions I do not know how to express directly. Suppose I say, 'The third sentence on page 42 of Jones's *Ichthyology* is true', and the third sentence on page 42 makes an ichthyological claim I lack the concepts to assert directly. I have managed to assert that proposition indirectly, by way of the indirect truth attribution.

This is not to say that minimalism avoids *all* the problems of the other varieties of deflationism. The explanatory problem and the evidentiary problem remain. The following seems correct:

(24)   The proposition that water is wet is true because water is wet.

But this is something minimalism cannot easily accommodate. A claim such as that one requires an explanatory connection between water's being wet and the truth of the proposition that water is wet. It is hard to see how any such explanatory connection could be accounted for using just the PES and its instances.

The evidentiary problem is similar. Consider again (3), 'The third sentence on page 42 of Jones's *Ichthyology* is true', supposing that the sentence in question is (4), 'Some pelagic fish are ovoviviparous'. There seems to be a great deal that would count as evidence in favor of (3) that would not count as evidence in favor of (4). Given minimalism, the effect of asserting 'The third sentence on page 42 of Jones's *Ichthyology* is true' is to assert all the instances of:

(25)   If the third sentence on page 42 of Jones's *Ichthyology* says that _, then _.

Many of those instances are vacuously true (i.e., the instances that fill the '_'s with a sentence that is not asserted by the third sentence on page 42). But, given that (4) is the third sentence on page 42 of Jones's *Ichthyology*, the instance of (25) that matters is this one:

(26)   If the third sentence on page 42 of Jones's *Ichthyology* says that some pelagic fish are ovoviviparous, then some pelagic fish are ovoviviparous.

And, given that that is what the third sentence on page 42 says, the only evidence we could have for (26) must be evidence that some pelagic fish are ovoviviparous. The trouble is that the sorts of things that might make us accept (3) concern such matters Jones's reliability and the publishing history of *Ichthyology*, which are not evidence that any pelagic fish are ovoviviparous.

6.5 Resolving the Explanatory and Evidentiary Problems

The three versions of deflationism surveyed above each face versions of the explanatory and evidentiary problems. Those problems, though, involve some assumptions about explanation and evidence that a deflationist of any stripe can (and perhaps should) reject.

The explanatory problem arises from the idea that deflationists cannot account for how the following claim:

(27)   Water is wet.

is true *because* water is wet. This is because deflationists treat 'It is true that water is wet' as equivalent to (27), and so saying (27) is true because water is wet then amounts to giving the following unacceptable explanation:

(28)   Water is wet because water is wet.

Nevertheless, deflationists can explain a thin sense in which (27) *is* true because water is wet, while denying that there is any legitimately more robust sense that their theory needs to account for.

Here is how one such account might go. We start by considering another kind of 'because' claim that makes sense and seems correct:

(29)   Jack is a bachelor because he is an unmarried man.

On one reading, of course, (29) is unacceptable as an explanation of Jack's bachelorhood. He can't be a bachelor *because* he is an unmarried man; that's the same as saying he's an unmarried man because he's an unmarried man. But there is another reading. Explanations are answers to 'why' questions, and the relevant 'why' question might be 'Why does the term 'bachelor' apply to Jack?'. An acceptable answer to that question could be an explanation that specifies what features of Jack make the word apply to him.

Now suppose that a "citizen" is defined to be someone who *either* was born in the country *or* has been naturalized. Imagine that Alice was born in the country, and Bob has been naturalized. Again, it is perfectly sensible, and not circular, to say that Alice is a citizen *because* she was born in the country, and to say that Bob is a citizen *because* he has been naturalized.

Both patterns of explanation involve pointing out a sufficient condition for a term to apply to something. In the first case, we point out a sufficient condition for the term 'bachelor' to apply to Jack. In the second, we point out the sufficient conditions (which happen to be different in the two cases) for 'citizen' to apply to Alice and to Bob. A deflationist can say that this is the only legitimate sense in which (27) is true because water is wet. The rules that govern our usage of 'true' mandate that it applies to (27) if, and only if, water is wet. And, since water *is* wet, 'true' applies to (27). No more substantive explanation (such as one that talks about correspondence or coherence) is needed.

Now let us turn to the evidentiary problem. For that problem to have any bite, we must suppose that evidence for 'The third sentence on page 42 of Jones's *Ichthyology* is true', given that that sentence is 'Some pelagic fish are ovoviviparous', is not evidence that any fish are ovoviviparous. But that supposition itself can be called into doubt.

What is evidence for what depends largely on what a person already knows. Suppose I am unsure whether there are any ovoviviparous pelagic fish, but I am aware that the Jones's *Ichthyology* says there are. In this case, any evidence I can gather about the reliability of Jones's text will help to justify me in accepting Jones's claim about ovoviviparous fish. From this point of view, evidence that Jones is reliable, and thus evidence that the third sentence on page 42 is true, really is evidence for me in favor of the claim that some pelagic fish are ovoviviparous.

Now suppose I am one of the expert reviewers of Jones's book. In this case, I would be doing my job badly if I took such things as Jones's reputation or the number of previous editions of the book as evidence that some pelagic fish are ovoviviparous. I would want to know what evidence there is, independent of Jones's saying so and the publication history of the book, for or against that claim, and I would want the sort of evidence ichthyologists use. Notably, though, in such a case, considerations of Jones's reputation and the previous editions of the book aren't evidence that the third sentence on page 42 is true either! In this case, all I could hope for by way of evidence that the sentence is true would be evidence that there are some ovoviviparous pelagic fish.

With respect to the evidentiary problem, then, a deflationist can simply stick to her guns and insist that, in any particular circumstances, a person's evidence that the third sentence on page 42 is true is exactly the same as that person's evidence that some pelagic fish are ovoviviparous. What can make it look otherwise is a failure to be clear about the epistemic situation of the person whose evidence we are considering. When such things as reputation and publishing history are relevant evidence for the truth of the third sentence on page 42, they are also relevant evidence for the existence of ovoviviparous pelagic fish. And when the only relevant evidence for the existence of such fish is the sort that ichthyologists accept in their capacity as ichthyologists, that is also the only relevant evidence for the truth of the third sentence on page 42.

6.6 Deflationism, the Equivalence Principle, and Realism

It is time to consider how deflationism fares with respect to the Equivalence Principle and realism. Deflationism's relationship to the value of truth will be discussed in the next section.

Of our desiderata, deflationism's relationship to the Equivalence Principle is the clearest. The redundancy theory delivers the T-biconditionals readily, since it considers 'It is true that _' to mean the same as the sentence that fills the blank. Consequently, 'It is true that _ if, and only if, _' means the same as '_ if, and only if, _', which is obviously correct if we fill the blanks with a non-paradoxical sentence. According to disquotationalism, 'It is true that _' is logically equivalent to the sentence that fills the blank. That comes to the same thing as saying that the instances of 'It is true that _ if, and only if, _' are logically true, much as 'Something is ... if, and only if, it is not the case that nothing is ...' is logically true. And for minimalism the connection between the theory of truth and the T-biconditionals is even closer. The very concept of truth is constituted by our acceptance of the instances of the Propositional Equivalence Schema. Rather than starting with a substantive theory of truth and aiming to derive T-biconditioanls, minimalism starts with T-biconditionals and then finds no further need for a substantive theory of truth.

What about realism? There is some reason to think that disquotationalism and the redundancy theory might have trouble explaining how claims could be true but unknowable. There may be some claims that cannot be known because it is not possible for us to understand them. This is not because the claims are nonsense, but rather because of our cognitive limitations. Predictably, it is quite difficult to come up with an example of such a claim, but we can try. Some philosophers (particularly Colin McGinn), have argued that there is a true solution to the mind/body problem, but it is in principle impossible for anyone to understand it and thus in principle impossible for anyone to know it. There are some sentences that are perfectly in keeping with the rules of English grammar, but that are too long and complex for anyone to parse in the finite amount of time between the Big Bang and the Big Crunch. There may be claims whose shortest statement is one of those sentences. If P is one of those claims, we cannot possibly know that P because we cannot possibly understand it.

If the truth predicate applies only to sentences one understands, then we seem committed to a variety of anti-realism. Rather than saying that only *knowable* claims can be true, though, this version says that only *understandable* claims have truth values. The limits of reality are not the limits of our knowledge, but the limits of our ability to grasp the meanings of claims. On this kind of view, McGinn's position that the mind/body problem has a true but incomprehensible solution would turn out to be a simple contradiction. There can't be such a solution, because only what we can understand is capable of being true.

There are two natural responses. The first is simply to bite the bullet and accept the anti-realist implications. The variety of anti-realism in question is much milder than the anti-realism discussed in Chapter 2, after all. It allows for the possibility of unknowable truths, so long as they are expressed by claims we can understand. It says only that our concepts of truth and falsehood fail to apply to claims we cannot understand. But since we are unable to understand those claims, and unable even to *express* them, we are equally unable to reason with them, to consider what follows from them, or to consider what they follow from. It might seem pretty harmless to withhold truth values from such claims.

Additionally, one might even describe this mild anti-realism, which denies truth values to claims we cannot understand, as in fact a kind of mild *realism*. On deflationism, we are guaranteed that:

(30) It is true that _ if, and only if, _.

holds for any (non-paradoxical) claim we can understand. It is much easier to understand a claim, though, than to know whether it is true or false. Take Goldbach's Conjecture:

(31) Every even number greater than 2 can be expressed as the sum of two prime numbers.

The Conjecture is easy to understand, but mathematicians have worked on the problem for more than 250 years without discovering a proof or disproof of it. The Conjecture might turn out to be neither provable nor refutable, making it and its denial unknowable. Nevertheless, it is easy for a deflationist who accepts the classical logical law of excluded middle and an equivalence schema for falsehood (i.e., 'It is false that _ if, and only if not-_') to prove that the Conjecture has a truth value:

(32) Let 'GC' be a name for Goldbach's Conjecture.
(33) By the logical law of excluded middle, either every even number greater than 2 is the sum of two prime numbers,

or not every even number greater than 2 is the sum of two prime numbers.

(34) By the Equivalence Principle for truth, GC is true if, and only if, every even number greater than 2 is the sum of two prime numbers.

(35) By the Equivalence Principle for falsehood, GC is false if, and only if, not every even number greater than 2 is the sum of two prime numbers.

(36) From (33), (34), and (35) above, it follows that either GC is true or GC is false.

Similar reasoning might establish that any unknowable claim we can understand is either true or false. (This is why anti-realists often reject classical logic's law of excluded middle, which says every claim is either true or false.) A deflationist who takes this line can deny truth values to claims we could not understand, while still allowing that unknowable claims we can understand have truth values after all. This sort of deflationist's position would be no different from an ordinary realist's view, with respect to the claims we can understand. Their only disagreement would concern claims we cannot understand. Given the impossibility of understanding those claims, a deflationist might wonder how a more thorough realist can be so sure the claims have truth values.

There are some reasons we might need truth values for claims we cannot understand. Let's take the case of Peano Arithmetic again, for example, and suppose that all the theorems of Peano Arithmetic are true. There are infinitely many such theorems, and some of them are inexpressible by any sentences any person could ever be in a position to parse or understand. But if the truth predicate only applies to sentences we can understand, and we cannot understand all the sentences that follow from the axioms of Peano Arithmetic, we are forced to conclude that not all the theorems of Peano Arithmetic are true after all.

The trouble isn't only with Peano Arithmetic. We tend to think that, if you accept some claims as true, then you are rationally bound to accept as true whatever follows from those claims as well. It is a contradiction to say, "Yes, it is entailed by some true claims, but it isn't true." Yet we must also admit that pretty much any set of beliefs that is very rich at all is bound to entail, through repeated application of logical laws we accept, some incomprehensible claims. We thus seem committed to the truth of those claims, even though we cannot understand them.

This introduces the second response a deflationist realist might have to the problem of claims we cannot understand. She could look for ways of extending the "core" concept of truth, which applies only to sentences one understands, to apply to other sentences as well. For example, she could allow that sentences we don't understand, but that follow from sentences we *do* understand, will have truth values. There may be still other sentences, so remote from us that not only are they incomprehensible to us, but they do not even follow from any sentences we can comprehend. A realist deflationist might even extend the core concept of truth to those sentences, at least far enough to say that such a sentence would have a truth value, but by hypothesis we have no idea what it would mean for such a sentence to be true or false.

6.7 Deflationism and the Value of Truth

The problem of accounting for the value of truth can be especially difficult for deflationists. It's not that deflationists can't hold that truth is the aim of belief or that it is better, other things being equal, to believe a true claim than to believe its denial. Rather, given a deflationist understanding of truth, it might seem very hard to explain why such things would be so.

Let us focus on the claim that it is better, other things being equal, for one to believe a true claim than to believe its denial. On any version of deflationism, this claim is to be interpreted as asserting all at once the collection of all the instances of the following schema (which we can call the "Value Schema"):

(37) If _, then it is better (other things being equal) to believe that _ rather than not-_.

Among the instances of this schema are such sentences as these:

(38)　If Chingachgook is the last of the Mohicans, then it is better (other things being equal) to believe that Chingachgook is the last of the Mohicans rather than that he is not.

(39)　If water is solid at room temperature, then it is better (other things being equal) to believe that water is solid at room temperature rather than that it is not.

(40)　If there is life on Mars, then it is better (other things being equal) to believe that there is life on Mars rather than that there is not.

(41)　If every even number greater than 2 can be expressed as the sum of two primes, then it is better (other things being equal) to believe that every even number greater than 2 can be expressed as the sum of two primes rather than that some are not.

and so on.

Deflationists have something to say about why we accept the instances of the Equivalence Schema. Each version of deflationism offers a view of how the logic of the truth predicate makes the instances of the schema logical truths on par with 'If Jack went up the hill, then Jack went up the hill' or 'All roses are roses'. But how can they explain our accepting the *Value* Schema's instances?

The most obvious reason one might give for accepting all the instances of the Value Schema is to appeal to the generalization that it is better to believe truths than their denials. That generalization, along with the relevant instances T-biconditionals, would enable us to derive any instance of the Value Schema that we want. For example, given these:

(42)　If a claim is true, then (other things being equal) it is better to believe that claim than to believe its denial.

(43)　'Diamonds are forever' is true if, and only if, diamonds are forever.

we can easily derive:

(44) If diamonds are forever, then it is better (other things being equal) to believe that diamonds are forever than to believe that diamonds are not forever.

Deflationists cannot give that explanation, though. On their view, the generalization that it is better to believe truths than their denials is just a way of expressing the instances of the Value Schema. Given the deflationist's own commitments, then, it would be circular to use that generalization to explain why the instances of the Value Schema are acceptable. That is, if we accept (42) because we accept all the instances of (37), we can't use (42) to explain why we accept (37).

Deflationists deny that all true claims have anything substantial in common, in virtue of which they are true. There is no robust property of truth that makes claims good to believe. Instead, deflationists often hold, it's the wetness of water (rather than the truth of a claim) that makes it good to believe that water is wet, it's the primeness of 7 (and not the truth of a proposition) that makes it good to believe that 7 is a prime number, and so on. A deflationist cannot consistently hold that the two claims are good to believe because they are made good to believe by the property, *truth*, that they have in common.

This problem and some of its relatives pose what may be the most significant challenge for deflationism. It is a large part of what motivates the "pluralist" theories of truth discussed in the next chapter. There are, however, some possible deflationist strategies for responding to the problem.

The problem arises only if we accept the generalization that it is better, other things being equal, to believe true claims than their denials. A deflationist could simply refuse to accept this claim, on various grounds. She might contend that the 'other things being equal' qualification is vague to the point of meaninglessness. Or, the deflationist could say that it *isn't* better, other things being equal, to believe true claims than their denials.

Although the second approach might seem quite implausible at first, it can be refined. First, the deflationist isn't saying it is better to believe falsehoods than truths, but only that it is not better, other things being equal, to believe truths than their denials. Second, the deflationist can put the 'other things being equal' clause to important use. It might be the case that, ordinarily, believing a true claim pays off more, in terms of successfully accomplishing the rest of what a person wants, than believing its denial would. But if *other things are equal*, then we must suppose that the costs and benefits of the beliefs in question are *exactly the same*. And, if I suppose it makes no difference to anything else I care about whether I believe some true claim or its denial, then it is much easier to imagine that it is no better to believe one than the other; it quite literally makes no difference.

It should be obvious that this approach would involve rejecting the view that truth is valuable for its own sake. The general strategy is to identify truth's value with the instrumental value of true beliefs, and thereby to give a principled reason to deny the generalization that it is, other things being equal, better to believe truths than their denials. Still, though, one might suspect a relative of this problem is still lurking in the neighborhood: How could a deflationist account for the generalization that it is ordinarily more beneficial to believe truths than their denials, given that deflationists must treat that as a way of expressing the instances of a schema such as (45) below?

(45)   Ordinarily, if _, then it is more beneficial to believe that _ than to believe that not-_.

It seems more promising for deflationists to make a pair of moves. The first is to treat generalizations such as 'Other things being equal, it is better to believe true claims than their denials' as telling us something about *belief*, rather than telling us something about *truth*. We should not expect a theory of truth to explain why that generalization holds. We should see the value of truth in belief as pertaining to the nature of belief, and so we should develop theories of the nature of belief that are able to account for why it is better to believe truths than their denials. For such a theory to be useful to a deflationist, though, it must *also* be compatible with deflationism. In particular, the theory of belief should not presuppose that truth is a substantive property whose nature goes beyond the logic of the truth predicate. This is a tall order, and it is an open question whether deflationists can fill it at all.

The second move is similar to the first, but it does not draw on a theory of the nature of belief. Instead, it focuses on the telic value of truth (see Chapter 3), and it aims to establish that we benefit from having a disposition to accept instances of the Value Schema. Rather than giving a philosophical explanation of why all the instances of the Value Schema are true, we might give a psychological explanation of why we are so deeply and stubbornly inclined to accept any instance of the schema. We might be wrong to accept some of those instances, and right to accept others. But because we are so strongly inclined to accept them, the generalization that it is better to believe truths than their denials strikes us as correct as well.

Some people will not find this approach persuasive. They will contend that we need an explanation for why the generalization holds, not an explanation for why we are so strongly inclined to accept it. A deflationist who takes this approach, though, is refusing to grant from the outset that the generalization holds. It certainly *seems* to hold, but the deflationist who makes the telic value move has an explanation for why that would be. This would put the onus on the objector to give some positive reasons in favor of the generalization, without begging the question against deflationism.

Further Reading

Ramsey's classic elaboration of the redundancy theory is (Ramsey 1927). Quine takes the disquotationalist approach in several places, including (1970) and (1992). His discussions also elaborate the relationship between disquotationalism and Tarski's project, a topic not explored in this chapter. The essays in Field (2001) include work on Field's versions of disquotationalism and his efforts to grapple with the problem of attributing truth to sentences one does not understand. Horwich outlines and defends his minimalism in

(1998), and Anil Gupta (1993) offers some important criticisms of it. Gupta makes some influential criticisms of deflationism in general in (2010).

Philip Kitcher (2002) argues that deflationists cannot account for the connection between true belief and successful action. For a defense of deflationism against Kitcher's objection, see Wrenn (2011).

See Künne (2003) for detailed discussions and criticisms of the varieties of deflationism. The *Stanford Encyclopedia of Philosophy* entries, "Truth" (Glanzberg 2009) and "The Deflationary Theory of Truth" (Stoljar & Damnjanovic 2012) also contain very good discussion, as well as very useful bibliographies.

Much work on deflationary theories of truth is driven by the problem of how to handle paradoxes such as that posed by a claim such as 'This claim is not true'. A good introduction to those issues is Burgess & Burgess (2011), and Beall (2009) explores a novel way of understanding the paradoxes from within an essentially deflationist framework.

7
Pluralist Theories of Truth

7.1 Truth Monism and Truth Pluralism

All the theories of truth surveyed so far are *monistic* in the sense that they treat the truth predicate as doing essentially the same thing whenever it is used. According to correspondence and coherence theories, to call a claim true is to attribute a certain property to it – viz., the property of corresponding to the world or of cohering with a suitable set of claims. Deflationary theories assign the truth predicate a certain logical function. To call a claim true, according to them, is to say something equivalent to the claim itself.

Recently, some philosophers have been exploring the prospects of an approach to truth that is *pluralistic* rather than monistic. There are two main varieties of pluralism. One is *simple pluralism*, sometimes associated with the work of Crispin Wright. According to simple pluralism, the truth predicate attributes different properties in different "discourses" or subject matters. If we call scientific claims true, we may be attributing a property much like correspondence to them. But if we call moral claims or claims about what is funny true, we are attributing a different property, which may be more like what coherentists have had in mind. The second form of pluralism is *alethic functionalism*, which has been most vigorously defended by Michael Lynch. According to view, for a claim to be true is for it to have a property that plays the "truth role," and different properties can play that role in different discourses.

This chapter describes some considerations motivating pluralism, and it outlines some of the more specific advantages and disadvantages of simple pluralism and alethic functionalism. It also evaluates pluralism in terms of the Equivalence Principle, the value of truth, and its commitments with respect to realism and anti-realism.

7.2   The Scope Problem Again

Epistemic and correspondence theories of truth have an important weakness in common, the *Scope Problem*. Consider these four claims:

(1) The mean distance between the earth and the sun is 96 million miles.
(2) *Ghostbusters* is a funnier movie than *Schindler's List*.
(3) It is wrong to allow suffering one could easily have prevented.
(4) The mirror didn't break, but it could have.

We can sensibly call any of these claims true or false. An epistemic theory of truth might seem plausible if we concentrate on claims such as (2) or, perhaps, (3). That's mainly because anti-realism is plausible for such claims; it is hard to imagine that something could be funny or wrong if there were no minds to appreciate their humor or wrongness. On the other hand, epistemic theories seem implausible if we concentrate on a claim such as (1). The distance between the sun and the earth seems to be entirely independent of our ability to measure it. A correspondence theory of truth seems to do well with (1) but poorly with (2), (3), or (4).

The Scope Problem for a theory of truth is the problem of apparently working well for some cases and poorly for others. Correspondence theories work well for the cases epistemic theories handle poorly, and vice versa, but neither approach seems to work well for all cases. Their failure to accommodate all the cases we want a theory of truth to explain is a serious weakness for both approaches.

Let us consider in more detail how the Scope Problem plays out. On an epistemic theory of truth, there is a very close connection between the truth of a claim and our ability to know it. Part of what it means for a claim to be true is that we could, under appropriate circumstances, know it. Thus part of what it means for (1) to be true is that we could, under appropriate circumstances, know that the earth is 96 million miles from the sun. The bad news for epistemic theories, of course, is that our ability to *know* how far the earth is from the sun seems to have no bearing on how far the earth *is* from the sun. Whether it is true or false that the earth is 96 million miles from the sun seems to be completely independent of whether or not there are any minds; had there been no minds, it would still be true (or false) that the earth is 96 million miles away from the sun.

An epistemic theorist's usual response is to embrace a far-reaching anti-realism and insist that truth depends on knowability even for a claim such as (1). If (1) is true, such a theorist will insist, it is true because we can know it. The problem, though, is that it is much more intuitively obvious that the distance between the Earth and the sun is mind-independent than that any epistemic theory of truth is correct.

On a correspondence theory, it might be easy to account for the truth of (1), but (2), (3), and (4) pose more difficult problems. The correspondence theorist must either deny that those claims are capable of being true (or false), or else explain what sorts of things those claims correspond to. Of the three, (2) might be easiest to accommodate. Perhaps people have laughed more often while watching *Ghostbusters* than while watching *Schindler's List*, and maybe that is the feature of the world that (2) corresponds to. Even that might not be fully satisfying, though, since it is far from clear that '*Ghostbusters* is a funnier movie than *Schindler's List*' means the same thing as 'People have more often laughed while watching *Ghostbusters* than while watching *Schindler's List*'.

Claims (3) and (4) present an especially acute problem for causal correspondence theories. On a causal correspondence theory, the truth of (3) requires the existence of a property, *wrongness*, that (a) is possessed by acts of allowing preventable suffering and (b) *causes* us, in the right way, to use the word 'wrong' to describe those acts. Although we might be able to explain how some properties, such as *having a negative charge* or *being a rabbit*, help to cause us to apply certain terms, it is very hard to see how moral properties such as *wrongness* fit into the causal order. This leaves causal correspondence theorists with a dilemma: either attribute mysterious causal powers to moral properties, or deny that claims like (3) really are meaningful and subject to being true or false. Neither option is very good. A similar dilemma arises with respect to counterfactual claims such as (4). We must either deny the claims have truth values after all, or we must find some way to reduce claims about what did not happen but could have to claims about what actually happened. Again, neither route looks promising.

Deflationism does not face the Scope Problem, because deflationists do not treat the truth predicate as attributing a property to claims. To call (1) true is to say the earth is 96 million miles from the sun; it is not say anything about the knowability of (1) *or* to assert that (1) bears a substantive correspondence relation to the world. To assert (2) is to say that *Ghostbusters* is funnier than *Schindler's List*. We can ask the further question of why the former is the funnier movie, or what, in general, it takes for one movie to be funnier than another, but those are questions the theory of truth does not prejudge, and in calling (2) true we do not take a side in those debates. The same goes for (3) and (4). There may be substantive issues about the nature of wrongness, but calling (3) true is just a way of calling it wrong to allow preventable suffering; it is not to take a side on substantive issues of meta-ethics. Likewise, to call (4) true is to say that the mirror did not break but could have, without thereby taking any position on the metaphysics of counterfactuals.

Its avoidance of the Scope Problem is a major advantage for deflationism over correspondence and epistemic theories, but pluralists think deflationism has other problems that make it an unacceptable theory of truth. The pluralist alternatives are meant to avoid the Scope Problem while *also* avoiding the further problems pluralists find with deflationism.

7.3   Two Problems for Deflationism

Crispin Wright has argued that deflationism is unstable. On his view, if one takes deflationism seriously, one must ultimately admit that the truth predicate serves more than a merely logical function after all; it attributes a property. Wright's argument draws on considerations of the normativity of truth. It is fairly intricate, but worth spelling out in some detail.

One of the central ideas in Wright's argument is the idea of *warranted assertibility*. For a claim to be warrantedly assertible is for it to be appropriate, given the available information, for one to assert that claim. For example, if the available evidence indicates that the cat is on the mat, then 'The cat is on the mat' is warrantedly assertible. If the available evidence does not indicate that the cat is on the mat, either because it indicates the cat is elsewhere or it is insufficient to tell us anything about where the cat is, then 'The cat is on the mat' is not warrantedly assertible. When a claim is warrantedly assertible, we can call the assertion of that claim *justified*.

Wright sees deflationism as committed to these two central and defining claims:

(5)   The truth predicate is a purely logical or grammatical device; the effect of calling a claim true is the same as what one would accomplish by asserting the claim itself. (Wright 1992, p. 14)

(6)   The Disquotational Schema (i.e., "P' is true if, and only if, P') provides virtually everything that is needed to explain the function of the truth predicate. (Wright 1992, p. 14)

We can call (5) the *Principle of Semantic Descent*, and we can call (6) the *Equivalence Schema Principle*. Wright thinks (5) and (6) commit deflationists to an inconsistent view, according to which truth and warranted assertibility both are and are not two different "norms of assertion."

A "norm of assertion" is a way in which an assertion can be correct or acceptable. Clearly, warranted assertibility is a norm of assertion. If the assertion of a claim is warranted by the available information, then that is a reason to assert the claim, or to accept or endorse its assertion. It is a way in which the assertion is correct or right.

It might seem obvious that truth is a second, and different, norm of assertion. Not only can an assertion be correct in the sense of being properly supported by the evidence, but it can be correct in the sense of accuracy or getting it right about the world. If a claim is true, then that is a reason to assert it, or to accept or endorse its assertion.

Given the Equivalence Schema Principle, it looks as though there are bound to be some claims that are true without being warrantedly assertible. Suppose, for example, that we have no information on the cat's whereabouts. Then neither of these claims is warrantedly assertible:

(7)   The cat is on the mat.
(8)   The cat is not on the mat.

Nevertheless, either the cat is on the mat or the cat is not on the mat, and the Equivalence Schema Principle is enough to give us these T-biconditionals:

(9)   'The cat is on the mat' is true if, and only if, the cat is on the mat.
(10) 'The cat is not on the mat' is true if, and only if, the cat is not on the mat.

Wherever the cat may be, either (7) is true or (8) is, and whichever one of them is true isn't warrantedly assertible.

That is how Wright argues that deflationists are committed to seeing truth as a different norm of assertion from warranted assertibility. They can't be the same norm, because a claim can be true without being warrantedly assertible. However, he argues that deflationists are *also* committed to seeing truth as the *same* norm of assertion as warranted assertibility. That is why Wright thinks deflationism is ultimately inconsistent.

Wright thinks deflationists must see truth and warrant as the same norm because, he says, we would assert exactly the same claims – and accept, endorse or allow the assertion of exactly the same claims – if we decided which claims to assert on the basis of truth or on the basis of warrant. Suppose you are trying to decide whether to assert that the cat is on the mat, and you are making your decision on the basis of whether it is true. That is, you intend to assert it if it is true, and not to assert it if it isn't true. You could make your decision only by considering the evidence and how well it supports the claim that the cat is on the mat. If it supports it well enough to justify you in thinking the claim is true, you will assert the claim. Otherwise, you will not.

Thanks in part to the T-biconditionals, though, you are justified in believing it is true that the cat is on the mat in *exactly* the same circumstances that you are justified in believing the cat is on the mat. So, you will judge 'The cat is on the mat' to be true in exactly the same cases that you would judge it to be warrantedly assertible. Whether you decide what to assert based on considerations of truth or of warrant, you will make exactly the same assertions.

Wright thinks the T-biconditionals and the grammar of the truth predicate alone provide no way to explain how truth and warrant could be different kinds of correctness when we are bound to count exactly the same claims correct in both senses. So, he thinks, deflationists must see truth and warrant as the *same* form of correctness, the same norm of assertion. That, however, contradicts deflationism's commitment to the view that truth and warrant are two *different* forms of correctness.

There are some potentially serious lines of objection to Wright's argument, which I will put off discussing until the next chapter (see Section 8.4). Instead, let us look at a second objection to the deflationary view, pressed by Michael Lynch as he develops his own version of pluralism.

Like Wright, Lynch is motivated in part by reflecting on the normative aspects of truth. In particular, he thinks it is centrally important to the very concept of truth that (a) truth is the aim of belief and (b) that truth is valuable. Moreover, and perhaps even more importantly, he thinks that the concept of truth must play a certain important explanatory function. Deflationism, he thinks, is incompatible with any of these things.

Let us begin with the idea that truth is the aim of belief. The idea is that there is a kind of success or failure that is particular to the having of beliefs, which we mark with words like "correct" or "incorrect." Just as a move in a game of chess might be "correct" or "incorrect" with respect to the goal of winning the game, beliefs are correct or incorrect with respect to a certain goal or aim. A belief is correct, of course, when it is true, and it is incorrect when it is false.

As Lynch sees it, this is not simply a matter of snow's whiteness making it correct to believe that snow is white, grass's greenness making it correct to believe that grass is green, and 17's primeness making it correct to believe that 17 is a prime number. Rather, there is a notion of correctness that applies to our beliefs irrespective of their contents and that is importantly *the same* for any two correct beliefs, whatever they might be. To make sense of the idea of correct or incorrect belief, we need to identify some property or feature that all and only correct beliefs have in common. That feature, Lynch thinks, is truth (2009b, p. 112).

Why might we think there is a single feature that all and only correct beliefs have in common? Suppose you acquire a new belief – say, the belief that:

(11)　Some pelagic fish are ovoviviparous.

That belief might be correct or incorrect, but we know what it means for the belief to be correct *even without* knowing what (11) means. That is important to Lynch because, if I don't know what (11) means, I can't know that:

(12)　A belief that some pelagic fish are ovoviviparous is correct if, and only if, some pelagic fish are ovoviviparous.

but I *can* know that:

(13)　A belief that some pelagic fish are ovoviviparous is correct if, and only if, it is true.

On a deflationary view, though, (13) is equivalent to (12), and so deflationism seems to be committed to something impossible – namely, that one can know (12) without being able to entertain the idea that some pelagic fish are ovoviviparous. On the other hand, if truth is a real property, shared by all and only correct beliefs, there is no problem. I may not know what (11) means, but I know a belief with that content is correct if, and only if, it is true.

Lynch also thinks deflationism is unable to account for the role the concept of truth plays in explanations. Two kinds of explanation are especially important here. One is in explanations of *meaning*. According a very popular philosophical understanding of meaning, to explain what a declarative sentence means is to explain the conditions under which it is true and the conditions under which it is false. This is called giving the "truth conditions" for the sentence. But now consider the relationship between the truth conditions of these two sentences:

(14)   Snow is white
(15)   There are cookies in the cookie jar.

If we suppose truth is a robust property, then there is something important those truth conditions have in common. Snow's being white is necessary and sufficient for 'Snow is white' to have that robust property, and there being cookies in the cookie jar is necessary and sufficient for 'There are cookies in the cookie jar' to have *the very same* property. We understand the meanings of sentences in terms of their relationship to the property of truth. On deflationism, though, truth cannot play such an explanatory role. There need not be anything interesting in common between one sentence's relationship to its truth conditions and any other sentence's relationship to its own truth conditions.

The concept of truth also seems to play a role in the explanation of our successful actions. Suppose you and I have an appointment to meet at Chuck's Café at 3:00. I have a true belief about the time and location of our meeting, and the truth of that belief is important to explaining how we succeed in meeting. A deflationary version of that explanation would simply say that we succeed because (a) we have an appointment to meet at Chuck's at 3:00, and (b) I believe we have an appointment to meet at Chuck's at 3:00. What that explanation leaves out is that, if our appointment had been at a different time or place, and my belief had still been true, we *also* would have succeeded. The deflationary explanation depends on the particular details about when and where I believe we are due to meet. It cannot account for the fact that, apart from those details, the truth of my belief plays a role in our success.

Though deflationists can respond to these objections (see the previous chapter and the next one), Lynch thinks the general theoretical situation is this: Epistemic and correspondence theories face the Scope Problem, but deflationism fails to do justice to the idea that truth is a kind of correctness and to the explanatory function of the concept of truth. He believes a certain kind of pluralist conception of truth can avoid those problems.

7.4   Simple Pluralism and Wright's View

The most straightforward way to try to solve the Scope Problem is *simple pluralism*. On simple pluralism, truth's nature is different for different subject matters. Sometimes truth is correspondence, and sometimes it is epistemic in some way. Even W. V. Quine, who ordinarily advocated disquotationalism, once remarked that, in science, something like a correspondence theory of truth applies, but ethics requires a coherence theory (Quine 1981).

Crispin Wright's version of pluralism is an elaboration of simple pluralism's basic idea. He offers an account of what it takes for a property to be truth for a given subject matter or, in Wright's term, "discourse." Additionally, he aims to do this while taking into account the normative dimension of truth revealed by his argument for the instability of deflationism.

Wright's strategy is to identify a number "platitudes" about truth, including these (1992, p. 34):

(16)   To assert a claim is to present it as true.
(17)   If a claim is capable of being true or false, it has a negation that is likewise capable of being true or false.

(18) To be true is to correspond to the facts.
(19) A statement may be justified without being true, and vice versa.

Some clarification of (18), the platitude that truth is correspondence to the facts, is in order. It is not an assertion of a correspondence theory of truth. Recall from Chapter 5 that there is a sense of "correspondence" that is uncontroversial, and neutral among all theories of truth. In that sense, "corresponds to the facts" is just another expression for "is true," and it does not commit one automatically to a metaphysics of facts or a particular correspondence relation. It is this second, uncontroversial sense, that is relevant to the platitude.

Any property that satisfies the platitudes for a given discourse is a truth property for that discourse, Wright thinks. It is perfectly possible that different properties are truth for different discourses. Two possible truth properties that Wright discusses are *superassertibility* and what I will call "robust correspondence."

A claim is *assertible* when there is some state of information we could be in that would justify asserting it. Note, though, that a claim could be assertible even though there is also an *improved* state of information we could be in that would not justify asserting it. For example, given only the information that Jones said she'd be in Vancouver this week, I might be justified in asserting that Jones is in Vancouver. But, if I also saw Jones touring the Alamo in San Antonio, Texas, the improvement in my information would undermine any justification I had for asserting that Jones is in Vancouver.

A claim is *superassertible* when, not only is there a state of information that would justify its assertion, but its assertion would remain justified no matter how that state of information was enlarged or improved (Wright 1992, p. 47). For some discourses, superassertibility might satisfy the platitudes. Wright's example is comedy; let us see how superassertibility could satisfy (13)–(16) and thus function as a truth property for discourse about what is funny. In particular, consider the claim that Bill's joke is funny.

It is implausible that a joke could be *unknowably* funny or *unknowably* unfunny. Something is funny if, and only if, it is possible to know it is funny. Furthermore, any claim that is knowable is also superassertible. Wright shows that these things imply that Bill's joke is funny if, and only if, it is superassertible that Bill's joke is funny. This seems to be enough to show that superassertibility satisfies (18), the correspondence platitude (properly construed).

The claim that Bill's joke is funny could be justified without being superassertible. I might have heard that Bill told the joke to a crowd of people who all laughed riotously, only later to hear the joke myself, not be amused, and learn that the original audience had a taken a drug that makes them respond to pretty much anything as if it were funny. Since a claim can be justified without being superassertible, superassertibility seems to satisfy (19).

Superassertibility applies to declarative sentences, and any declarative sentence is capable of being superassertible or not. This is why superassertibility satisfies (17), the platitude that anything capable of being true or false has a negation that is also capable of being true or false.

Finally, let us consider (16), the platitude that to assert something is to present it as true. If someone asserts that Bill's joke is funny, have they presented it as superassertible? Wright thinks it is possible. The key is that, when one makes an assertion, one presents oneself as having information that justifies that assertion. So, one presents the claim as *at least* assertible. Furthermore, if one expected future improvements in one's information to undermine one's justification in asserting the claim, then one would not be justified in asserting it *now*. If I expect to learn later that Bill's joke wasn't funny, then I am not justified in asserting now that it is funny. This last point can be strengthened. Not only must I not expect future information to undermine my justification, I must expect any future information *not* to undermine my justification. If I thought my justification might be undermined in the future, I shouldn't say flatly that Bill's joke is funny. I should say something more cautious instead, such as 'Bill's joke seems funny' or 'Bill's joke is probably funny' or 'So far as I can tell, Bill's joke is funny'. Consequently, if I do flatly assert that Bill's joke is funny, I am presenting the claim that Bill's joke is funny as not only warrantedly assertible, but *durably* so. I am presenting it as superassertible.

Even if superassertibility is truth in some discourses, it may not be truth in all discourses. For discourses where realism seems appropriate, something beyond superassertibility is called for. Goldbach's Conjecture might be unprovably true. In that case, it is not superassertible, even though it is true. Some claims about the state of things distant in time or space might not be superassertible, yet they might still be true. In such discourses, truth seems to be something more than mere superassertibility. It is something else, deserving of the name "robust correspondence."

Robust correspondence is the kind of relation that correspondence theorists have in mind. It is what the dictum that truth is correspondence to the facts refers to when we understand it as saying more than simply that a claim is true when (and only when) things are as it says they are. Robust correspondence involves two important ingredients, the correspondence relation, and the facts or states of affairs in the world to which true claims correspond.

Why might we think truth for a discourse (such as science, for example) is robust correspondence rather than mere superassertibility? Wright discusses several reasons, but one of the most important ones is this. Consider the states of affairs a discourse appears to concern itself with, e.g., what things are funny, what things are morally correct, how much heat is generated by chemical reactions, tomorrow's weather, etc. What role do those states of affairs play in explanations? What sorts of things does the funniness of Bill's joke explain? Here are some possibilities:

(20) The funniness of the joke explains why everyone thinks it is funny. (Maybe – unless the joke is funny because everyone thinks it is.)

(21) The funniness of the joke explains why everyone laughed at it. (Indirectly – they laughed because they thought it was funny, and they thought it was funny because it was.)

(22) The funniness of the joke explains why the cops showed up at the party. (Indirectly – the cops showed up in

response to a neighbor's complaint about the noise from the people laughing at the funny joke.)

Notice that, in every case, the funniness of the joke either explains people's judgments about its funniness, or, if it explains something else, it does so *indirectly*, by way of explaining people's judgments about it.

Contrast a case in which we might be tempted to be realists, the claim that it rained all night last night. Not only might last night's rain explain some people's beliefs to the effect that it rained last night, but it can also explain other things, such as:

(23)   The creek is spilling over its banks because it rained all night last night.
(24)   There is a puddle at the end of the driveway because it rained all night last night.
(25)   The plants in the garden are well watered because it rained all night last night.
(26)   The earthworms have crawled onto the patio because it rained all night last night.

and so on. Its having rained last night explains a fairly wide array of things, independently of its relationship to our believing it rained last night. When a discourse appears to deal with such states of affairs, Wright thinks, we have reason to think of truth in that discourse as going beyond mere superassertibility and, instead, involving a robust relation of correspondence to mind-independent facts.

Wright's overall case for pluralism thus has several parts. First, Wright thinks deflationism is unable to do justice to the idea that we aim for our assertions to be not only justified but true, and that these are two different aims. Second, he thinks that there are some areas of discourse, such as discussions about what is funny, where truth seems to be epistemic, and others, such as discussions of scientific matters of fact, where truth seems *not* to be epistemic but more like what the correspondence theorists say it is. The best view, he thinks, is that there are some discourses in which truth is epistemic and others in which it is some form of correspondence. His view is even open to the possibility of a more thorough pluralism, where even epistemic truth varies from discourse to discourse, and correspondence truth does the same.

7.5   Simple Pluralism, Mixed Compounds, and Mixed Inferences

Simple pluralism, even as elaborated by Wright, faces two very serious problems. These problems motivate Lynch to reject Wright's style of pluralism, and his "functionalist" type of pluralism is designed specifically to resolve them.

The first is the problem of "mixed compounds." Suppose, as Wright invites us to, that truth is superassertibility for claims about what is funny, but truth is correspondence for claims about the atomic numbers of elements. A mixed compound is a sentence that combines claims from two or more different discourses. An example of a mixed compound is the following sentence:

(27)   The one about the nun at the dude ranch is very funny, and the atomic number of gold is 79.

What is truth for a compound like (27)? The sentence is a conjunction. It is true if, and only if, both its parts are true. This means the above sentence is true if, and only if, it is true that the one about the nun at the dude ranch is very funny, and it is also true that the atomic number of gold is 79.

Suppose truth for such a compound is correspondence. Then the conjunction will be true if, and only if, both its parts have the property of *correspondence truth*. Even though 'The atomic number of gold is 79' might have that property, 'The one about the nun at the dude ranch is very funny' does *not* have that property. It is part of a discourse in which there is no such thing as corresponding to a fact or not; truth in that discourse is epistemic. So, if truth for the compound is correspondence, then it seems the compound will be inevitably false.

So then suppose that truth for such compounds is superassertibility. It is plausible that both 'The one about the nun at the dude ranch is very funny' and 'The atomic number of gold is 79' are superassertible. So far, so good. But what if we substitute something unknowably true for the second conjunct? For example, what are we to do with compounds like this one?

(28)   The one about the nun at the dude ranch is very funny, and there is an inhabited planet outside the light cone of earth.

(I am assuming it is true and unknowable that there is such a planet. If that's not the case, then substitute any other unknowable truth.) Now we have what amounts to the same problem as before. Even if 'The one about the nun at the dude ranch is very funny' is superassertible, 'There is an inhabited planet outside the light cone of earth' is not. Consequently, the claim seems doomed to falsity regardless of whether or not there is an inhabited planet outside earth's light cone.

The trouble with mixed compounds is that they combine sentences from discourses with different truth properties, and there is no satisfactory way to decide which discourse's version of truth applies to the compound. One reasonable way to try to avoid the problem is to stipulate that mixed compounds do not belong to the discourses of their constituents, but to some other discourse with its own variety of truth. For example, one might adopt a view that says (i) truth about comedy is superassertibility, (ii) truth about atomic numbers of elements is correspondence, (iv) truth for mixed compounds is a complex property constructed out of superassertibility and correspondence along the following lines:

(29)   If P is a claim about comedy and Q is a claim about chemistry, then 'P and Q' is true if, and only if, both P is superassertible and Q robustly corresponds to the facts.
(30)   If P is a claim about comedy and Q is a claim about chemistry, then 'P or Q' is true if, and only if, either P is superassertible or Q robustly corresponds to the facts.

and so on.

Let's suppose that a strategy like that can work. Then we will run into another problem (which has been lurking in the background all along) – the *problem of mixed inferences*. Consider the following two arguments (Tappolet 1997):

(31) *Wet Cats*
P1 Wet cats are funny.
P2 Tabby is a wet cat.
C Therefore, Tabby is funny.

(32) *Nuns and Numbers*
P1 The one about the nun at the dude ranch is very funny.
P2 The atomic number of gold is 79.
C Therefore, the one about the nun at the dude ranch is very funny, and the atomic number of gold is 79.

In a mixed inference, the premises come from different discourses. "Wet Cats" infers a conclusion about what is funny from a premise about what is funny and a premise about Tabby's being wet (for which a pluralist is apt to say that truth is correspondence). The conclusion of "Nuns and Numbers" is a mixed compound, and that argument's premises also come from two different discourses.

Intuitively, both inferences are valid, and valid inferences are supposed to be *truth preserving*. The usual (non-pluralist) definition of truth preservation is simply that, when an inference is truth preserving, the truth of all its premises logically guarantees that the conclusion is also true. Some philosophers, such as Lynch, think it is important to the idea of truth preservation that valid inferences "preserve" truth in a literal sense. We must be guaranteed that, if the premises have a truth property, then the conclusion has *the very same* truth property.

The premises of "Wet Cats" have two different truth properties. There is thus no single truth property that can be preserved when we infer the conclusion from them. But if there is no such property, the inference is not truth preserving and thus not valid, and therein lies the problem. "Wet Cats" is valid, and our theory of truth should not require us to say it is not.

"Nuns and Numbers" also has premises with different truth properties. Unlike "Wet Cats," though, its conclusion is a mixed compound. While the truth property for the conclusion of "Wet Cats" is at least the same as the truth property for one of its premises, the truth property for the conclusion of "Nuns and Numbers" is not the same as the truth property for *either* of its premises. The upshot is the same as before: There is no truth property preserved in the transition from premises to conclusion, and so the argument appears to be invalid. But the argument is valid, and our theory of truth should not say it isn't.

7.6 Alethic Functionalism

Lynch's response to the problems of mixed compounds and mixed inferences is *alethic functionalism*. The basic idea of his theory is that there is a single property of truth, but that there are many *ways* of being true or, to use Lynch's preferred terminology, many different ways of *manifesting* truth. In some discourses, truth might be manifested by superassertibility; in others, it might be manifested by causal correspondence. In still others, it might be manifested by what Lynch calls "concordance," which is a kind of coherence. Truth is manifested in mixed compounds by a complex property we can define in terms of the properties that manifest truth in the constituents.

There are two important features of this view. First, for any given discourse, there is a distinctive way in which claims can be true, but claims in different discourses need not be true in the same way. This is the sense in which Lynch thinks "truth is many." However, all these ways of being true are still ways of *being true*. The various properties that manifest truth are all manifesting a single property, the property of truth. This is the sense in which Lynch thinks "truth is one."

Three other cases, which have nothing to do with truth, can help clarify how alethic functionalism is supposed to work. First, consider the role of Hamlet. Many different actors have played Hamlet, including Kenneth Branagh, Sir Lawrence Olivier, Mel Gibson, Keanu Reeves, Sarah

Bernhardt, and Richard Burbage. Different people play the role in different productions of *Hamlet*. Nevertheless, it is a single role all these people are playing. Just as Hamlet is a role that different actors might play in different productions, the alethic functionalist thinks of truth as a role that different properties might play in different discourses.

A second analogy is to be found in the relationship among the properties *being red*, *being crimson*, and *being scarlet*. *Being crimson* is not the same property as *being scarlet*, but both are ways of being red. Concordance and correspondence are not the same property either, but both (in suitable discourses) are ways of being true.

A third analogy, from which Lynch derives the name "alethic functionalism," draws on the functionalist view in the philosophy of mind. According to functionalism, a mental property, such as the property of *being in pain*, can be realized in different ways in different sorts of creatures. For example, pain might be realized in mammals by a certain kind of brain activity – call it brain activity X. Imagine there are Martians without brains, who have green goop in their feet that performs all the same functions as mammalian brains do. Pain for Martians is realized by a property of their goop; call it goop property Y. Mammalian pain is brain activity X, while Martian pain is goop property Y, but both are *pain*, and when a mammal and a Martian are both in pain, they really do have a property in common. Similarly, truth in one discourse might be concordance, and it might be correspondence in another, but any two true claims do have a property in common, the property of *truth*.

Alethic functionalism is designed to preserve the insight of simple pluralism while avoiding the problems of mixed compounds and mixed inferences. It avoids the problem of mixed compounds by allowing that what manifests truth for them is a complex property incorporating the properties that manifest truth in their components. It avoids the problem of mixed inferences by distinguishing between truth and the properties that manifest truth. Valid inferences need not preserve what manifests truth in the transition from premises to conclusion. Rather, what must be preserved is truth itself, the property of having a property that plays the truth role. The truth of the premises of "Wet Cats" guarantees that its conclusion will have a property that plays the role of truth. The truth of the premises of "Nuns and Numbers" likewise guarantees that its conclusion will have a property that manifests truth, even though two different properties manifest truth in the premises' home discourses and a third property manifests truth for the conclusion.

Just as the simple pluralist owes an account of what makes a property truth for a discourse, the alethic functionalist owes an account of what it takes for a property to play the truth role in a discourse. Like Wright, Lynch approaches this problem by way of what he takes to be "platitudes" about truth. He does not give a comprehensive list of all such platitudes, but he does think there are a handful of "core" platitudes, including:

(33) *Objectivity*. The belief that p is true if and only if, with respect to the belief that p, things are as they are believed to be.
(34) *Norm of Belief*. It is *prima facie* correct to believe that p if and only if the proposition that p is true.
(35) *End of Inquiry*. Other things being equal, true beliefs are a worthy goal of inquiry.

Lynch thinks of the platitudes as giving a rough "job description" for truth, but he does not think a property has to satisfy all the platitudes to manifest truth for a discourse. Rather, he thinks, whatever property *best* satisfies the platitudes within a discourse is that discourse's manifester of truth. It is not perfectly clear what it means for a property to best satisfy the platitudes, but a good first approximation is probably that the property that satisfies the *most* platitudes, especially the core platitudes, for the claims in a discourse is the property that manifests truth for that discourse.

7.7 Objections to Pluralist Theories of Truth

Pluralism is designed to avoid the Scope Problem while maintaining the idea that the truth predicate expresses a more-than-merely-logical property. Nevertheless, it faces several problems of its own. Among the most important are the problem of individuating discourses, the charge of metaphysical extravagance, and the inheritance of weaknesses of other theories of truth.

To "individuate" discourses is to specify the conditions under which two different sentences are part of the same discourse or part of two different discourses. Intuitively, we might suppose that 'Gold has an atomic number of 79' and 'Wet cats are funny' belong to different discourses, and we might suppose that 'Lead is a chemical element' belongs to the same discourse as 'Gold has an atomic number of 79'. But there are certainly hard cases. Consider 'Torturing cats is cruel' and 'Torturing cats is wrong'. Are they members of the same discourse as 'Wet cats are funny'? On the one hand, all three sentences are about cats, so they seem to be part of cat-discourse. But on the other hand, there is no philosophical consensus as to whether evaluations of things as funny are of the same kind as evaluations of things as cruel or wrong. Are aesthetic and moral judgments simply species of something more general, "value judgments," or are they different in ways important enough to make talk about morality and talk about comedy into different discourses, with potentially different truth properties? There is room for philosophical debate about whether the idea of wrongness is built into the idea of cruelty. If it is, then 'Torturing cats is cruel' and 'Torturing cats is wrong' might belong to the same discourse. If it is not, though, 'Torturing cats is cruel' might turn out to be a morally neutral description of cat torture, and it might be part of a non-moral discourse after all.

Both simple pluralism and alethic functionalism maintain that different properties can be (or manifest) truth in different discourses. Both Wright and Lynch go to some lengths to spell out what it takes for a property to be truth for a discourse, but it is not clear what makes a claim belong to one discourse rather than another. Lynch (2009b, pp. 79–81) says it is a matter of the kind of concepts that constitute the claim, but he offers no account of what makes a concept belong to one "kind" or another. (See also (Williamson 1994) for a version of this objection.)

There are at least two ways this is a problem for pluralism. First, and most generally, the notion of a discourse is a centrally important part of the pluralist approach to truth. One should expect, then, for pluralists to have something to say about what makes a collection of claims count as a discourse, and what makes a claim belong to one discourse rather than another. Otherwise, pluralists will have simply replaced the problem of explaining what makes claims true or false with the problem of explaining what makes them belong to one discourse rather than another. That might not be progress.

Discourse individuation poses a second sort of problem for pluralism if we suppose that understanding a sentence requires knowing the conditions under which it is true. Given pluralism, we cannot know the conditions under which a sentence is true unless we first know what discourse it belongs to and what constitutes truth for that discourse. Imagine that (a) truth is correspondence in purely descriptive discourses, and (b) it is superassertibility or concordance in moral discourse, but (c) we are unsure which discourse includes 'Torturing cats is cruel'. Until we can decide what discourse it belongs to, we can't know what is required for 'Torturing cats is cruel' to be true. Consequently, we can't understand the sentence without already knowing what discourse it belongs to.

This seems to get things exactly wrong. The supposition that understanding a sentence requires knowing its truth conditions is extremely plausible as a theory of understanding, and we seem to be able to understand 'Torturing cats is cruel' perfectly well, even without taking a position on whether moral wrongness is intrinsic to cruelty or on whether truth is something other than correspondence in moral discourse. Pluralism appears to require us to know too much before we can understand a sentence.

A pluralist might respond that this objection conflates the ordinary concept of truth with its underlying, pluralistic metaphysics. To apply the concept of truth, I need only understand the core platitudes. Comprehending (or accepting!) the pluralistic metaphysics of truth is not necessary for me to apply the concept, just as I need not comprehend (or accept) anything about chemistry in order to competently apply the concept *water*. The pluralist might contend that grasping the truth conditions of a claim is simply a matter of applying the ordinary concept of truth, not applying a metaphysical theory of truth. That is, we can grasp the truth conditions of 'Torturing cats is cruel' without having to decide whether those are conditions for the claim to correspond to the world, for it to be superassertible, or whatever.

This reply may not help the pluralist much. If we can know the truth conditions of 'Torturing cats is cruel' without knowing whether they are conditions of correspondence, superassertibility, concordance, or whatever, then what *do* we know when we know the claim's truth conditions? All that is left, once we have eliminated knowledge of what would manifest truth in the claim's home discourse, appears to be something like this:

(36) 'Torturing cats is cruel' is true if, and only if, torturing cats is cruel.

That, however, seems to be a concession to deflationism. It allows that we can use the truth predicate to explain what is involved in understanding a claim *without* thereby committing ourselves to any metaphysical theory of the nature of truth.

The most natural pluralist move in response to the problem of discourse individuation is to turn the order of explanation around. What makes two claims belong to the same discourse is that the same truth property applies to both of them. Although this does distinguish discourses from one another, it does not help us to figure out what truth property applies to a given claim. We could not start by seeing what discourse the claim belongs to, because we could only assign claims to discourses by *first* figuring out what truth property applied to them. To decide whether 'Torturing cats is cruel' belongs to a moral or descriptive discourse, for example, we would first have to figure out whether its truth would be a matter of correspondence, superassertability, concordance, or something else. This approach might solve the problem of assigning claims to discourses, but it would deprive pluralism of an advantage as well. If we explained discourse membership in terms of what property constitutes truth for individual claims, it would be circular to explain what property constitutes truth for an individual claim in terms of what discourse it belongs to.

Pluralism also faces a problem of metaphysical extravagance (Sainsbury 1996). Consider again the claims that gold's atomic number is 79 and that wet cats are funny. The pluralist holds that truth is not the same property for these two claims. Instead, chemical truth is a different property from aesthetic truth. Non-pluralists, especially deflationists, are apt to reply that pluralism posits more different properties than are needed to get the explanatory work done. According to their objection, the difference between the property of *having the atomic number 79* and the property of *being funny* suffices to explain everything that needs explaining. *Having the atomic number 79* is the sort of property something could have even if no one ever thought about it and even if no minds had ever existed. *Being funny* is the sort of property something can have only in virtue of its relationship to people's minds. Given the differences between these properties, we don't need to suppose that truth is two different properties for the two different claims. Truth could be disquotational in both cases, or it could even be a form of correspondence in both cases – 'The atomic number of gold is 79' corresponds to the state of affairs that gold atoms have 79 protons, and 'Wet cats are funny' corresponds to a state of affairs involving the relationship between wet cats and people's minds.

To answer the metaphysical extravagance objection, pluralists would need to give a reason to suppose the differences between such properties as *being funny* and *having atomic number 79* do not account for the supposed differences between such discourses as comedy and chemistry. It is currently unclear whether pluralists can meet this challenge.

A final problem for pluralism derives from the way it piggybacks on other theories of truth. Take Lynch's functionalist view. Lynch thinks causal correspondence manifests truth in science, but concordance (a more demanding variety of coherence) manifests truth in moral discourse. Lynch's account thus inherits many of the problems of the causal correspondence view and the coherence theory of truth.

Many of those problems have been surveyed in previous chapters. For example, the causal correspondence view has trouble handling counterfactuals and claims involving 'because'. It relies on a causal theory of reference, which makes it hard to account for the truth of claims involving numbers (including that thoroughly scientific claim that $E = mc^2$!), and it also has difficulty explaining just what "the right" reference-fixing causal connections are.

Coherentism suffers the problem of alternative coherent systems. At first, one might think it is harmless to allow that different and incompatible systems of belief about what is funny are equally true. But the harmlessness might not withstand scrutiny. Take 'Wet cats are funny'. Suppose it coheres with Alice's beliefs about what is funny, and it does not cohere with Bob's. We might *say* it is true for Alice but not for Bob, but really it seems that we have given up on evaluating it as true or false at all. Saying it is true for Alice just means it coheres with what she already believes, and saying it is true for Bob just means it coheres with what he already believes. That is well and good, but unless I share Alice or Bob's system of beliefs about comedy, the news that 'Wet cats are funny' is true for Alice only tells me something about Alice. It does not tell me anything about the humorousness of wet cats.

The problem of alternative systems also applies to Lynch's view that moral truth is concordance. We need not get into the details of what concordance is here, apart from mentioning that (i) there is a sense in which concordance allows for *fewer* alternative systems than ordinary coherence does, but (ii) concordance does not rule out alternative, mutually inconsistent, equally concordant systems of belief altogether. But as long as it allows for *at least two* such alternative systems, the problem is a real problem. If I know 'It is wrong to torture cats' is concordant with Alice's system and not with Bob's, then that does not yet tell me anything about the wrongness of torturing cats rather than just some psychological facts about Alice and Bob. It doesn't give me a reason not to torture cats. Moreover, if it should turn out that, for *any* given moral claim, there is a concordant system of beliefs that includes it and another, equally concordant system that includes its denial, then we seem to be left with a form of moral relativism that ultimately takes moral discourse out of the truth game altogether.

7.8   Pluralism's Scorecard

In evaluating any theory of truth, we should consider not only its inherent strengths and weaknesses, but its relationship to the issues of realism and anti-realism, the Equivalence Principle, and the value of truth. Pluralism's most prominent defenders, Wright and Lynch, take those issues very seriously, and their views are designed to do well on such a scorecard.

Start with the issue of realism and anti-realism. Wright's work is based on the important insight that, in addressing that issue, we really are interested in particular families of claims. We want to know whether the claims of science, or of morality, are mind-independent. We can address those issues by way of considering whether, for a given discourse, it is necessary to think of truth as more than just superassertibility. Lynch is interested in defending a position that is realist about science but, when it comes to ethics, is neither realist nor denies truth values to moral claims.

Pluralism gives Wright a way to frame the question of realism versus anti-realism, and thus a way to address it particular discourse by particular discourse, rather than at a higher level of abstraction or generality. Pluralism tolerates different resolutions of the realism/anti-realism issue in different arenas. Perhaps realism is true *of science* but anti-realism is true *of comedy*. Pluralism also gives Lynch precisely what he is looking for. It allows him to make sense of the idea that truth sometimes requires correspondence and sometimes does not, even though it is always truth.

Within some limits, pluralism also fares well with respect to the Equivalence Principle. Pluralism holds that different discourses can have different truth properties. Truth for a discourse could be correspondence, superassertibility, coherence, or concordance, for example. Suppose X is truth for a given discourse. The equivalence:

(37)   The claim that P is X if, and only if, P.

is guaranteed to hold, *provided* X is truth for the discourse that includes P. If P belongs to a different discourse, the equivalence will not hold, but that is not worrisome for the pluralist. If P is part of a certain discourse, there is little reason to care whether it has some *other* discourse's truth property, and its having or lacking another discourse's truth property has no bearing on whether P is true.

Now let us consider how pluralism fares with respect to the normativity and value of truth. Wright and Lynch both hold that part of what makes a property qualify as truth for a discourse is that it is a property in virtue of which assertions or beliefs are correct, and its lack makes assertions or beliefs incorrect. Wright includes 'To assert is to present as true' as one of his platitudes, and Lynch includes 'Truth is the aim of belief' as a core platitude. These versions of pluralism thus have no problem accounting for truth's role as an aim of belief or assertion or for the sense in which true beliefs or assertions are better than false ones. Being valuable in this way is part of what makes a property a truth property, and part of what it means to call a claim true is to evaluate it as correct to assert or believe.

Pluralism treats truth as a normative property. Whether one takes this to be an advantage will depend on whether one is persuaded (by arguments such as Dummett's outlined in Chapter 3 or Wright's described in this chapter) that truth really is normative, rather than a non-normative property we have reason to care about. Pluralism does not say much directly about what *sort* of value truth has – intrinsic, instrumental, final, constitutive, or telic. Nevertheless, it does not appear to say anything that rules any of those possibilities out. Indeed, pluralism appears to be consistent with the idea that, in some domains, there is an instrumentally valuable property that is truth, while in others the property that is truth is intrinsically or telically valuable. It is even consistent with the possibility that some truth properties are only finally valuable, provided final value is a genuine kind of value after all.

Despite its internal problems, then, pluralism fares pretty well with respect to the standards against which we are measuring theories of truth. In light of the Scope Problem, the most plausible approaches to truth appear to be either deflationary or pluralist. The next chapter gives a glimpse of how one might defend a variety of deflationism from the pluralist challenge.

Further Reading

The *Stanford Encyclopedia of Philosophy* entry, "Pluralist Theories of Truth" (Pedersen & Wright 2013) is a nice overview of pluralism and its problems, and it includes a very useful bibliography. Also see Pedersen (2012) for a good overview of recent work.

Crispin Wright presses his objections to deflationism in the first chapter of *Truth and Objectivity* (1992). Another discussion of pluralism, and its relationship to other theories of truth is in Wright (2001). For an early formulation of Lynch's alethic functionalism, see Lynch (2001). Lynch's most extensive formulation and defense of his functionalism is in *Truth as One and Many* (2009b).

Mark Sainsbury (1996) argues that the Scope Problem may not be as serious as Wright and Lynch seem to think it is, suggesting that apparent differences between the ways in which 'Water is wet' and 'Compassion is praiseworthy' are true have to do with the differences between wetness and praiseworthiness, not variation in what truth itself involves. In his 2009 review of *Truth as One and Many*, Stewart Shapiro suggests that there may be multiple varieties of designation but only one kind of truth.

Problems of mixed compounds and mixed inferences have received much recent attentions, including Tappolet (1997), Sher (2005), Pedersen (2006), Edwards (2008), Cotnoir (2009), Lynch (2005a; 2009b).

8
Deflationism Revisited

8.1 Advancing the Debates

The preceding chapters have surveyed many different ways of answering the question, "What is truth?" Among contemporary philosophers, by far the most popular approaches are the causal correspondence theory and various forms of deflationism, but pluralism's popularity is on the rise. Adjudicating among these views requires weighing the advantages and disadvantages of each and comparing the merits of each to the others.

The main aim of this chapter is to show how we might continue to make progress in the debates over the nature of truth. The best way to do that, I think, is to actually engage those debates and try to contribute to them. That is why this chapter will set aside the pros-and-cons approach of the previous ones and, instead, take a more polemical turn. This chapter outlines some considerations that, in my view, help to show that a generally deflationary approach to truth is preferable to the causal correspondence and pluralist approaches. The arguments here certainly do not settle the issue for good and all, but they do help to shed light on some important issues in the contemporary debates.

The discussion begins with some common ground among deflationary, causal correspondence, and pluralist theories.

That common ground helps motivate a version of *methodological deflationism*, the view that we should accept deflationism unless and until we find that there is work the concept of truth must do that is not accounted for by the logic governing the truth predicate. Next, I argue that that the causal correspondence theory has no explanatory advantage over deflationism, and I argue that the reasons Crispin Wright and Michael Lynch have given for preferring pluralism to deflationism are insufficient. These arguments suggest that, if we are to find work for the concept of truth that requires more than deflationism provides, then we will need to keep looking.

8.2 Common Ground and Methodological Deflationism

Any plausible theory of truth will satisfy the Equivalence Principle. It will guarantee the correctness of the non-paradoxical T-biconditionals, such as:

(1) 'Grass is green' is true if, and only if, grass is green.

and:

(2) It is true that hydrogen is a metal if, and only if, hydrogen is a metal.

Those biconditionals, furthermore, are enough to account for the truth predicate's role in disquotation and generalization.
For example, given this T-biconditional:

(3) 'Snow is white' is true if, and only if, snow is white.

we can infer each of these from the other:

(4) Snow is white.
(5) 'Snow is white' is true.

That is how the truth predicate is able to play its disquotational role. We can use "Snow is white' is true', a sentence about a sentence, to say something about the whiteness of snow. The family of T-biconditionals also underwrites the truth predicate's role in generalizations. Generalizing over sentences and disquoting them with the truth predicate allows us to make claims about the world that we otherwise could not make, by making claims about sentences.

Since *any* plausible theory of truth will deliver this much, it is common ground for deflationists, causal correspondence theorists, and pluralists. Given the Equivalence Principle, it is not in dispute that the truth predicate can be a device for disquotation. Rather, deflationists disagree with advocates of the other views, whom we might call "inflationists," about whether the concept of truth does important work that requires more than disquotation and generalization. Deflationists say it doesn't; inflationists say it does.

The core idea of deflationism is that the logical function of the truth predicate – especially its role as a device of disquotation and generalization – is all there is to the nature of truth. The deflationary answer to "What is truth?" is not a philosophical theory of the nature of the property of truth, but rather something fairly trivial: Truth is being true, and a sentence is true when, and only when, things are as it says. As Chapter 6 illustrates, specific varieties of deflationism work out the details of this idea differently, but those details will not matter to the arguments of this chapter.

Methodological deflationism (Field 1994) is more modest than the deflationism described above. It does not assert that truth has no essence or that there is nothing more to the nature of truth than the logic of the truth predicate. Rather, methodological deflationism (at the outset, anyway) is silent on those issues. A methodological deflationist takes deflationism as a working hypothesis, trying to see what, if anything, we need an inflationary conception of truth for. It could turn out that there are important explanatory tasks deflationary truth cannot discharge but some other notion, such as pluralist truth or causal correspondence truth, can. If so, then we have a reason to suppose truth is more than what deflationism says it is. But the burden is on the inflationist. We should suppose deflationism is the correct approach to truth until we have compelling reason to think otherwise.

The deflationist might seem to be stacking the deck in her own favor by recommending we take deflationism as the default view, to be abandoned only when we have strong reasons to accept one of its rivals, but there is nothing unfair about it. All sides agree that the truth predicate is useful for disquotation and generalization. Let us call the logic of the truth predicate, which underwrites its role in disquotation and generalization, L. Deflationists basically just adopt L as their theory of truth, but an inflationary theory consists of L + X, where X is some additional set of claims that go beyond the logic of the truth predicate, whether those are the claims of the causal correspondence theory or the claims of a pluralist theory. If L alone accounts for all the work the concept of truth does, the addition of X would be a pointless, idle theoretical curlicue. This is why methodological deflationism makes sense. Methodological deflationism says, "Let's try to explain all we can with L alone, and then let's see if there is work that remains to be done. If so, we'll reject deflationism in favor of some inflationary rival. But if not, we'll stick with deflationism because we have no good reason to accept an inflationary view of truth."

8.3   Deflationism vs. the Causal Correspondence Theory

According to some advocates of the causal correspondence theory, the concept of truth does important *explanatory* work that (a) deflationary approaches cannot account for but (b) causal correspondence theories can. For example, Philip Kitcher (2002) has argued that the causal correspondence theory, but not deflationism, can explain the connection between true beliefs and systematically successful action. Given methodological deflationism, this would be a powerful reason to prefer the causal correspondence approach, if it were correct. A close examination of how causal correspondence theories work, though, suggests they can provide no explanations that are not already available to deflationists.

The causal correspondence theory has three parts. First is its causal theory of reference, according to which terms designate objects and properties in virtue of bearing certain very complicated causal relationships to those objects and properties. Second is its Tarski-style definition of truth in terms of designation. That definition relies on such clauses as:

(6)   An atomic sentence is true if, and only if, the object designated by its singular term has the property designated by its general term.

(7)   A sentence of the form 'P and Q' is true if, and only if, 'P' is true and 'Q' is true.

(8)   A sentence of the form 'Not-P' is true if, and only if 'P' is not true.

(9)   An existentially quantified sentence is true if, and only if, there is something that has the property its general term expresses.
      etc.

The third part of the causal correspondence theory is rarely mentioned. It is the claim that the first two parts of the theory characterize the essence of a substantial, not merely logical, property that carries significant explanatory weight. The causal correspondence theory is an inflationary theory, and its advantage over deflationism is supposed to be that causal correspondence truth can do explanatory work that deflationary truth cannot.

Not every version of the causal theory of reference is compatible with the causal correspondence theory of truth. For example, some causal theories of reference presuppose that truth is substantial property and explain reference in terms of truth and causation. It would be unacceptably circular to explain truth in terms of reference while explaining reference in terms of truth.

The causal correspondence theory needs a causal theory of reference with two important features. First, it must not already presuppose that truth is a substantial property. Second, it must provide a correct mapping from terms, on the one hand, to the objects and properties they designate, on the other. Clauses such as (6) of the Tarski-style truth definition rely on such a mapping, and the purpose of the theory of reference is to supply it.

Suppose we have a causal theory of reference with these features available, and consider what happens when we combine that theory of reference with a *deflationary* theory of truth. For concreteness, consider the version of deflationism whose "theory of truth" is just the collection of non-paradoxical instances of the schema:

(10)   S is true if, and only if, s.

where 'S' is replaced by a name for a sentence and 's' is replaced by that sentence (or, if necessary, its translation into English). The result is that the deflationist could then *derive* the Tarski-style truth definition that a causal correspondence theory relies on.

Here is how. Start with the T-biconditional:

(11)   'Hydrogen is a metal' is true if, and only if, hydrogen is a metal.

The causal theory of reference supplies these claims:

(12)   Hydrogen is the object designated by 'hydrogen'.
(13)   *Being a metal* is the property designated by '_ is a metal'.

Together, (11), (12), and (13) imply:

(14)   'Hydrogen is a metal is true' if, and only if, the object designated by 'hydrogen' has the property designated by '_ is a metal'.

This is an instance of a perfectly general pattern. Take any sentence of the form 'a is F'. Our deflationary theory of truth provides the T-biconditional:

(15)   'a is F' is true if, and only if, a is F.

The theory of reference tells us that a is the object 'a' designates and F is the property 'F' designates, and so:

(16) a is F if, and only if, the object named by 'a' has the property expressed by 'F'.

And (15) and (16) in turn imply:

(17) 'a is F' is true if, and only if, the object named by 'a' has the property expressed by 'F'.

But 'a is F' is any atomic sentence combining a singular term, 'a', with a general term, 'F'. Thus we can conclude:

(18) An atomic sentence is true if, and only if, the object denoted by its singular term has the property expressed by its general term.

and that is identical to (6) of the causal correspondence theorist's truth definition. A deflationist could derive the other clauses of the definition similarly.

A causal theory of reference useful to causal correspondence theorists would also be acceptable by deflationist lights, because it would not presuppose that truth is a substantive property. There are deflationary theories of reference on offer (see, e.g., Horwich (2010)), but nothing in deflationism *per se* requires denying that causal connections between names and individuals, or between predicates and properties, constitute designation. Furthermore, a deflationist who accepts such a causal theory of reference can also help herself to the clauses of the Tarski-style truth definition that a causal correspondence theorist accepts. This shows that deflationists can help themselves to the first two parts of the causal correspondence theory, without compromising their deflationism, the causal theory of reference and a Tarski-style truth definition.

It could turn out that we need those parts of the causal correspondence theory in order to give certain explanations, such as explanations of the relationship between true belief and successful action. So long as those explanations do not also depend on the third part of the causal correspondence theory (the claim that truth is a substantial property with a certain essence), though, they will be equally available to both causal correspondence theorists and deflationists. But are there explanations that require that further claim, the only part of the causal correspondence theory that is inconsistent with deflationism?

There is good reason to think not. The causal correspondence theorist's inflationary claim is that truth is a substantial property whose essence is given by the causal theory of reference and the Tarski-style truth definition. But if that claim is correct, it seems that whatever we might explain in terms of the truth we can also explain in terms of the causal theory of reference and the Tarski-style definition. There seems to be no further explanatory work left for the claim that they describe the essence of truth to do.

Compare the idea that the essence of being a bachelor is being unmarried and male. Everything explained by someone's bachelorhood is already explained by his being unmarried and male. Likewise, since the essence of being water is being composed of H_2O, everything explained by something's being water is explained by its being composed of H_2O molecules. This suggests that, if the causal theory of reference and the Tarski-style definition describe the essence of truth, then everything explained by something's being true is explained by the causal theory of reference and the Tarski-style definition. So, it seems, the third part of the causal correspondence theory does no distinctive explanatory work.

Given methodological deflationism, we should accept the causal correspondence theory only if there is important work for the concept of truth that (a) cannot be done with the deflationary conception of truth but (b) can be done with the causal correspondence conception of truth. The deflationary conception of truth is capable of doing any work that requires the first two parts of the causal correspondence theory, and there seems to be no explanatory work that requires the third part. If all that is correct, then the causal correspondence theory of truth does not have more explanatory power than the deflationary conception. Unless there is some heretofore unidentified, important, non-explanatory work the deflationary conception cannot do but the causal correspondence conception can, we should prefer the deflationary conception.

8.4 Deflationism vs. Pluralism

Pluralists believe different properties can "be" truth in different discourses. According to Wright's version, the truth predicate sometimes expresses one property and sometimes expresses another. According to Lynch's functionalist pluralism, truth is the property of having a property that plays a certain role in a discourse, and different properties play that role in different discourses. Given methodological deflationism, we should accept one of these views only if the concept of truth has a function pluralist truth can perform but that requires more than the mere logical function of the truth predicate provides.

Pluralists have pointed to two main kinds of work the concept of truth does that, they claim, require more from it than deflationism provides. First, Wright thinks we use the truth predicate to "register a norm" distinct from the norm of warranted assertibility (see Section 7.3). Second, Lynch (and many other critics of deflationism) thinks we put the concept of truth to work in certain kinds of explanations – especially explanations of meaning and explanations of successful action – that require supposing truth is a richer property than deflationism allows. Neither philosopher's objections to deflationism are convincing.

Let us begin with Wright's claim that deflationism cannot accommodate the fact that the truth predicate marks a distinct norm of assertion from warranted assertibility. We have two entirely different ways of evaluating assertions and judging them to be correctly made or not. One is to evaluate their warrant. In that case, we ask whether the available information is sufficient to justify believing what is asserted. The other is to evaluate their truth. In that case, we ask whether things are as the assertions say they are. Assertions can be "correct" in the sense of being warranted, or they can be "correct" in the sense of being true, but those are two different sorts of correctness. Some assertions are warranted without being true, and some are true without being warranted.

According to Wright, deflationists cannot consistently see the truth predicate as marking a kind of correctness different from warranted assertibility. As discussed in Chapter 7, this is because, on Wright's view, the T-biconditionals commit us to counting exactly the same assertions as warranted that we count as true. For example, consider the claim 'Snow is white' and the T-biconditional:

(19) 'Snow is white' is true if, and only if, snow is white.

If a person has good enough reasons to warrant asserting that snow is white, then, thanks to the T-biconditional, she has good enough reasons to warrant asserting that 'Snow is white' is true. It would be contradictory, after all, to assert that snow is white but 'Snow is white' is not true. Likewise, if a person has good enough reasons to warrant asserting that 'Snow is white' is true, she has good enough reasons to warrant asserting that snow is white. When it comes to evaluating assertions, then, we seem bound to evaluate a claim as warrantedly assertible if, and only if, we are willing to evaluate it as true. Since we are bound to evaluate the very same claims as true that we evaluate as warrantedly assertible, and the deflationist gives us nothing but the logic of the truth predicate to go by, deflationism seems unable to consistently count truth as a different sort of correctness from warranted assertibility.

To see the mistake in Wright's reasoning, we can begin by noticing it is sometimes perfectly sensible to count a claim as warrantedly assertible but false. Warranted assertibility depends on the information available to the person making the assertion. For a claim to be warrantedly assertible is for a certain person with certain information to be justified in asserting the claim, given that information. Warranted assertibility is, in that sense, relative. What is warrantedly assertible for one person at one time might not be warrantedly assertible for someone else at another. In the late seventeenth century, some chemists would have asserted this claim:

(20) When a substance burns, it emits phlogiston, a gaseous substance with negative mass.

They would have been warranted in making that assertion, given the information available to them at the time. They could see that burning substances emit gases, and the experimental evidence indicated that things weigh more after being burned than they did before. Nevertheless, we now know their claim was untrue. There is no such thing as phlogiston.

The seventeenth-century chemists' claim is an example of one that is warranted (for them, then) but not true. It highlights a crucial false assumption of Wright's argument. When we evaluate an assertion as warranted, we are not evaluating whether it is warranted for us, now, but whether it is warranted for those who made the assertion. The question of warrant is a question about the information available to the person making the assertion, or to her audience. The question of truth is different. Evaluating an assertion as warranted does not commit one to evaluating it as true, and the T-biconditionals do not have that consequence. If we evaluated the seventeenth-century chemists' assertion of (20) as warranted, then the T-biconditionals might require us to evaluate a seventeenth-century chemist's assertion of the following as warranted as well:

(21) 'Burning substances emit phlogiston' is true.

but that does not commit us to *believing* (20) or (21). It is perfectly consistent to hold that (21) is warrantedly assertible by seventeenth-century chemists while denying (20) and (21).

Granted, we are committed to counting as warranted *for ourselves right now*, given our present information, exactly the same claims we are prepared to call true, but the question of warrant and the question of truth are still different questions. To see a claim as warranted (for us, now) is to see it as supported by the information now available to us. It leaves open the possibility that others – including our future selves – with different information might not be warranted in asserting the claim. It is different to see a claim as true. It was true in the seventeenth century, for example, that combustion is a chemical process of rapid oxidation, not a process of releasing phlogiston, even though that assertion would not have been warranted in the seventeenth century.

Wright suggests that there is no difference between deciding what to assert on the basis of what is warrantedly assertible for one and deciding what to assert on the basis of what is true. Either way, all a person can do is to consider the information available and what assertions it warrants. There is a difference, though, that Wright does not fully appreciate. If I decide what to assert on the basis of what is warranted, without taking truth into account, then I will concern myself with whatever the prevailing standards of warrant are and the information that is currently available to me. I will assert claims that, according to my and my audience's standards, are sufficiently well supported by the available information. But I need not take any sort of critical attitude toward the standards in question. I need not take into account the possibility that my audience and I are employing standards that are unreliable in general, that will sanction the assertion of claims that later turn out to be false, or that fail to sanction the assertion of claims that later turn out to be true. If I am concerned with truth, though, I will care not only about whether what I assert satisfies my and my audience's standards of acceptability, but I will care about the quality of those standards themselves. I will consider how reliable the standards I am applying are, and I will aim to apply the most reliable standards I can.

Another example can illustrate the difference between concern for warrant and concern for truth. Suppose I said yesterday that Alice would be at Bob's party tonight, but I've just heard from Carol that Alice has made an emergency overseas trip to visit a sick relative. In light of the new information, I might retract my previous assertion that Alice would be at the party, on the grounds that it was not true. I have no reason, though, to stop seeing my past assertion as warranted. It was adequately supported by the evidence available to me at the time. Although the assertion was incorrect, its incorrectness was not a matter of inadequate evidential support. If I were concerned with warrant but not truth, I would have no reason to retract my earlier assertion. My assertion was warranted, and the emergence of new information doesn't change the fact that it *was* warranted, even if I would not be warranted in asserting it again now.

This sort of case indicates that we can retract previous assertions on either of two grounds: on the grounds that they were untrue, or on the grounds that they were unwarranted.

Moreover, that is perfectly consistent with deflationism. If we find out our evidence at the time did not support what we thought it supported, we might retract a previous assertion on the grounds that it was unwarranted. On the other hand, if we find out that what we asserted isn't so, we might retract it on the grounds that it is not true. There is plenty of room for deflationists to treat truth and warranted assertibility as distinct norms of assertion. If they were the same norm of assertion, then we should expect there to be no difference between retracting an assertion on the grounds that it was unwarranted and retracting it on the grounds that it was false. There is such a difference, and deflationists are in a fine position to characterize it. An unwarranted assertion is inadequately supported by the information available to the speaker, and a false one says that things are other than they are.

Let us turn now to Lynch's objections to deflationism. He contends that, if we confined ourselves to the disquoting and generalizing functions of the truth predicate, it could not play the role it does in explaining the meanings of sentences and the success of actions. He has in mind two different explanatory uses of the truth predicate:

(22) The truth conditions of many sentences explain their meanings.

(23) The truth of our beliefs often explains the success of our actions.

In (22), truth is supposed to play a "constitutive" role in explaining meanings (Lynch 2009b, p. 121). The truth conditions of sentences such as 'Snow is white' are part of what "constitutes" or, as Lynch sometimes says, "necessarily determines" their meanings. In (23), the idea is that true beliefs explain successful action because, other things being equal, we are more likely to get what we want when we believe the truth about how to get what we want (Lynch 2009b, p. 121).

There are two main ways we might try to understand the claim that truth conditions "constitute" or "necessarily determine" meanings. One, which is clearly mistaken, is that the relationship between truth conditions and meaning is something like the relationship between water and H_2O. Any sample of water is constituted by a collection of H_2O molecules. It is a sample of water by virtue of being so constituted, and it has its chemical properties because of the structure of H_2O molecules and the laws of chemistry that govern them.

If truth conditions constituted meanings in that sense, we should expect sentences to mean what they do *because* they have the truth conditions they have. That gets things exactly backwards, though. Even though we can learn a lot about meaning by looking at truth conditions, sentences do not have their meanings because they have the truth conditions they do. Rather, they have their truth conditions because of what they mean.

Take the German sentence, 'Der Schnee ist weiss', which is true if, and only if, snow is white. It also means that snow is white. It would be a mistake, though, to think 'Der Schnee ist weiss' means that snow is white because it is true if, and only if, snow is white. Rather, the explanatory arrow runs in the opposite direction. Why is 'Der Schnee ist weiss' true if, and only if, snow is white? Because it means that snow is white. Meaning explains truth conditions, not the other way around.

The second, more plausible, way to understand the claim that truth conditions constitute meanings is to see it as encapsulating this idea:

(24)   Necessarily, two sentences are alike in meaning if, and only if, they are alike in truth conditions.

On this interpretation, meaning "supervenes" on truth conditions, which is to say that there can be no differences in meaning without differences in truth conditions.

Claim (24), though, is exactly the sort of generalization deflationists see the truth predicate as enabling us to make. For two sentences, S_1 and S_2, to be alike in truth conditions is for the following to hold:

(25)   Necessarily, S_1 is true if, and only if, S_2 is true.

Thus, (24) tells us:

(26) Necessarily, two sentences, S_1 and S_2, are alike in meaning if, and only if: necessarily, S_1 is true if, and only if, S_2 is true.

In (26), the truth predicate is playing its usual role as a device for generalization and disquotation. We can see 'S_1' and 'S_2' as placeholders for names of sentences, and we can let 's_1' and 's_2' serve as placeholders for the respective translations of those sentences into our language. Thus (26) encapsulates all the instances of the schema:

(27) Necessarily, two sentences, S_1 and S_2, are alike in meaning if, and only if: necessarily, s_1 if, and only if, s_2.

Some of those instances (allowing for English-to-English translation) include:

(28) Necessarily, 'Der Schnee ist weiss' and 'Snow is white' are alike in meaning if, and only if: necessarily, snow is white if, and only if, snow white.
(29) Necessarily, 'Der Schnee ist weiss' and 'La neige est blanche' are alike in meaning if, and only if: necessarily, snow is white if, and only if, snow is white.
(30) Necessarily, 'Der Schnee ist weiss' and 'Grass is green' are alike in meaning if, and only if: necessarily, snow is white if, and only if, grass is green.

So, we need not go beyond what deflationism provides to capture the idea that meaning is constituted by truth conditions, interpreted as (24).

Lynch also thinks deflationists are unable to account for the way the truth of our beliefs helps to explain our practical success (2009b, p. 121). Truth appears to explain success in the following way: I am more likely to get what I want if I believe the truth about how to get what I want, and I am less likely to get what I want if I don't believe the truth about how to get it. Lynch thinks this must mean more than just the totality of claims like these:

(31)   I am more likely to get what I want if I believe that closing the door will get me what I want, and closing the door will get me what I want.
(32)   I am more likely to get what I want if I believe that changing jobs will get me what I want, and changing jobs will get me what I want.
(33)   I am more likely to get what I want if I believe that ordering another beer will get me what I want, and ordering another beer will get me what I want.

and so on. ...

What is missing, Lynch says, is the "counterfactual dependence" of my success on the truth of my beliefs:

> [B]y explaining the success of my actions in terms of the *truth* of my belief, I implicitly convey new modal information: I convey the information that *other* true beliefs would also have brought about success had the world been different than it is – even if, in fact, it had been ... different in ways I *cannot even imagine*. (2009b, p. 126, emphasis in original)

Not only am I more likely to succeed if I have true beliefs about how to get what I want, but, if things had been different, I would have been more likely to succeed if I had believed what was true about how to get what I wanted. The collection of claims such as (31)–(33) tells us nothing about how true belief would have helped me if things had been different.

This move of Lynch's is unfair to deflationism. Lynch looks at the deflationary understanding of:

(34)   I am more likely to get what I want if I believe the truth about how to get what I want.

and he faults it for not adequately capturing an idea we can express more explicitly as:

(35)   I am more likely to get what I want if I believe the truth about how to get what I want, and, if things were

different, I would be more likely to get what I wanted
if I believed the truth about how to get what I wanted.

There is a deflationary understanding of (35) as well. It
encapsulates not only the claims listed above, but also the
totality of claims like these:

(36) If things were different such that going to the concert
      were how to get what I wanted, then I would be more
      likely to get what I wanted if I believed that going to
      the concert were how to get what I wanted.
(37) If things were different such that eating twelve choco-
      late cakes were how to get what I wanted, then I would
      be more likely to get what I wanted if I believed that
      eating twelve chocolate cakes were how to get what I
      wanted.
(38) If things were different such that waking up earlier
      were how to get what I wanted, then I would be more
      likely to get what I wanted if I believed that getting up
      earlier were how to get what I wanted.

et cetera. ...

Deflationism can accommodate what Lynch calls the
"counterfactual dependence" of success on true belief
after all.

A defender of Lynch's view might respond that we want
some explanation of why there is a counterfactual link
between true belief and successful action. One possibility is
that truth is a property with a nature that goes beyond the
logical function of the truth predicate, and its nature determines that one would be more likely to succeed, even in
counterfactual cases, if one's beliefs were true. Compare the
case of the natures of water and salt. A given lump of salt
might never encounter any water, but the natures of water
and salt are such that, if the salt were to be immersed in
enough water for long enough, it would dissolve. We can
explain why certain counterfactuals are true by citing the
natures of the properties involved.

In this case, though, we do not need to cite the nature of
the property of *truth* to get the explanations we need. Instead,
we could cite the nature of belief. It seems to be part of the
nature of belief that, if you believe a claim, you are thereby

disposed to act as though the world is a certain way. You are disposed to act in ways whose success depends on the truth of your belief.

Imagine you see a dog chasing a squirrel, and the squirrel darts out of sight. The dog runs in the direction the squirrel went, and it begins to bark up a tree. We naturally say the dog believes the squirrel is in the tree, because the dog is behaving as though the squirrel is in the true. It is behaving in such a way that it is more likely to get what it wants if the squirrel is in the tree than otherwise. It seems to be part of the notion of belief that, when you believe something, it disposes you to act in ways whose success depends on the truth of what you believe.

A deflationist could happily allow that part of the nature of belief is that believing a claim disposes one to act in ways whose success depends on whether the claim is true. That generalization expresses the totality of claims such as these:

(39) Believing that a squirrel is in a tree disposes one to act in ways that are more likely to succeed if the squirrel is in the tree.

(40) Believing that water is a liquid disposes one to act in ways that are more likely to succeed if water is a liquid.

(41) Believing that closing the door is how to get what one wants disposes one to act in ways that are more likely to succeed if closing the door is how to get what one wants.

and so on. ...

Once we see this aspect of the nature of belief, we need nothing more than the generalizing and disquoting functions of the truth predicate to account for the counterfactual dependence of successful action on true belief. Lynch's claim to the contrary thus appears to be false.

Given methodological deflationism, we should prefer pluralist to deflationary accounts of truth only if there is important work the pluralist conception of truth can do but the deflationist conception cannot. Wright and Lynch's reasons for rejecting the deflationary conception in favor of a pluralist conception of truth appear to be insufficient. So far, then, the deflationary account has the advantage.

As we saw in Chapter 7, pluralism has problems of its own. Apart from those problems, though, is the fact that pluralism is unduly inflationary. The methodological deflationist perspective has modesty on its side. Let's not assume anything about the nature of truth, apart from the logical function of the truth predicate, unless we find that we must do so for some specific reason. The reasons pluralists such as Wright and Lynch give for thinking we need an inflationary notion of truth are insufficient. We have also seen that causal correspondence theories cannot have explanatory power beyond what deflationism provides. Pending new, better reasons for an inflationary view of truth, deflationism seems to be on very strong footing indeed.

8.5 Conclusion

What is truth?

This book has surveyed a variety of answers, emphasizing their advantages and disadvantages, with special attention to how they fare with respect to the Equivalence Principle, objectivity, and explaining the value of truth. If deflationism is correct, though, the question has a rather surprising answer. Truth is not a property with a nature we need to explain with a philosophical theory. Rather, the truth predicate is a logical device for generalization and disquotation. For a claim to be true is just for things to be as the claim says they are, and that is pretty much all there is to it.

I favor a deflationary conception of truth, and I have tried in this chapter to outline considerations that favor deflationism over causal correspondence and pluralist approaches. Much work remains to be done. Even if deflationist truth can do all the explanatory work of causal correspondence truth, the latter conception might be better suited to some other, non-explanatory task. Even if Lynch and Wright's criticisms of deflationism fail, there remain other important objections to the approach, including those discussed in Chapter 6. Answering such objections, or formulating a plausible version of deflationism that avoids them, remains among the most important items on deflationists' philosophical to-do list.

Furthermore, if methodological deflationism is correct, we should always be testing the limits of the deflationary conception of truth. We might find that there is important work it cannot do, and such a discovery would help us to see what sort of inflationary theory of truth we need.

A satisfying answer to the question, 'What is truth?', even a deflationary answer, needs to do certain things. It needs to deliver the non-paradoxical T-biconditionals. It needs to avoid implausible varieties of relativism and anti-realism, without falling into skepticism or implausibly strong varieties of realism. And it needs to account for the fact that the truth of our beliefs is worth caring about. The pursuit of an answer that does all those things well is an exciting, ongoing project of contemporary philosophy.

References

Aristotle. 1941. *The Basic Works of Aristotle*. Ed. Richard Peter McKeon. Random House.

Armstrong, D. M. 1997. *A World of States of Affairs*. Cambridge: Cambridge University Press.

— 2004. *Truth and Truthmakers*. Cambridge: Cambridge University Press.

Austin, J. L., P. F. Strawson, and D. R. Cousin. 1950. Symposium: Truth. *Proceedings of the Aristotelian Society, Supplementary Volumes* 24: 111–72.

Beall, Jc. 2009. *Spandrels of Truth*. Oxford; New York: Oxford University Press.

Blanshard, Brand. 1939. Coherence as the nature of truth. In *The Nature of Truth: Classic and Contemporary Perspectives*. Ed. Michael P. Lynch. Cambridge, MA: MIT Press, 2001.

Bradley, F. H. 1914. *Essays on Truth and Reality*. Cambridge: Cambridge University Press, 2011.

Brogaard, Berit and Joe Salerno. 2012. Fitch's paradox of knowability. In *The Stanford Encyclopedia of Philosophy*. Fall 2012 edn. Ed. Edward N. Zalta.

Burgess, Alexis and John P. Burgess. 2011. *Truth*. Princeton: Princeton University Press.

Cotnoir, Aaron J. 2009. Generic truth and mixed conjunctions: Some alternatives. *Analysis* 69 (3): 473–9.

David, Marian. 2013. The correspondence theory of truth. In Zalta, Edward N. (ed.), *The Stanford Encyclopedia of Philosophy* (Fall 2013 Edition), http://plato.stanford.edu/archives/fall2013/entries/truth-correspondence/.

De Houwer, Jan, Sarah Thomas, and Frank Baeyens. 2001. Association learning of likes and dislikes: A review of 25 years of research on human evaluative conditioning. *Psychological Bulletin* 127 (6): 853.

de Jong, Peter F., Willem Koomen, and Gideon J. Mellenbergh. 1988. Structure of causes for success and failure: A multidimensional scaling analysis of preference judgments. *Journal of Personality and Social Psychology* 55 (5): 718–25.

Descartes, René. 1641. *Meditations, Objections, and Replies*. Ed. Roger Ariew and Donald A. Cress. Indianapolis, IN: Hackett Publishing, 2006.

Dorsey, Dale. 2006. A coherence theory of truth in ethics. *Philosophical Studies: An International Journal for Philosophy in the Analytic Tradition* 127 (3): 493–523.

Dummett, Michael. 1958. Truth. *Proceedings of the Aristotelian Society* 59:141–62.

Edwards, Douglas. 2008. How to solve the problem of mixed conjunctions. *Analysis* 68 (2): 143–9

Engel, Pascal. 2002. *Truth*. Montreal: McGill-Queen's University Press.

— 2005. Truth and the aim of belief. In *Laws and Models in Science*. Ed. D. Gillies. London: King's College Publications.

Evans, J. D. G. 1974. Aristotle on relativism. *The Philosophical Quarterly* 24 (96): 193–203.

Field, Hartry. 1972. Tarski's theory of truth. *The Journal of Philosophy* 69 (13): 347–75.

— 1994. Deflationist views of meaning and content. *Mind* 103 (411): 249–85.

— 2001. *Truth and the Absence of Fact*. Oxford: Oxford University Press.

Frege, Gottlob. 1956. The thought: A logical inquiry. *Mind* 65 (259): 289–311.

Glanzberg, Michael. 2009. Truth. In *The Stanford Encyclopedia of Philosophy*. Spring 2009 edn. Ed. Edward N. Zalta.

Gott, J. Richard III, Mario Jurić, David Schlegel, Fiona Hoyle, Michael Vogeley, Max Tegmark, Neta Bahcall, and Jon Brinkmann. 2005. A map of the universe. *The Astrophysical Journal* 624 (2): 463–84

Gupta, Anil. 1993. Minimalism. *Philosophical Perspectives* 7: 359–69.

— 2010. A critique of deflationism. *Philosophical Topics* 21 (2): 57–81.

Harman, Gilbert. 1977. *The Nature of Morality*. Oxford, UK: Oxford University Press.

Hookway, Christopher. 2010. Pragmatism. In *The Stanford Encyclopedia of Philosophy*. Spring 2010 edn. Ed. Edward N. Zalta.

Horgan, T. and M. Potrc. 2000. Blobjectivism and indirect correspondence. *Facta Philosophica* 2 (2): 249–70.

— 2001. Contextual semantics and metaphysical realism: Truth as indirect correspondence. In *The Nature of Truth: Classic and Contemporary Perspectives*. Ed. Michael P. Lynch. Cambridge, Mass.: MIT Press.

Horwich, Paul. 1998. *Truth*. Oxford: Oxford University Press.

— 2010. *Truth-Meaning-Reality*. Oxford: Oxford University Press.

Hume, David. 1739. *A Treatise of Human Nature*. Ed. David Fate Norton and Mary J. Norton. Oxford: Oxford University Press, 2000.

— 1777. *Enquiries Concerning Human Understanding and Concerning the Principles of Morals*. Ed. L. A., Sir Selby-Bigge and P. H. Nidditch. Oxford: Clarendon Press, 1975.

James, William. 1907a. Pragmatism's conception of truth. In *Pragmatism and Other Writings*. New York, NY: Penguin, 2000.

— 1907b. What pragmatism means. In *Pragmatism: Classic and Contemporary Readings*. Ed. H. S. Thayer. Indianapolis, IN: Hackett Publishing, 1982.

Kant, Immanuel. 1781. *Critique of Pure Reason*. Ed. Paul Guyer and Allen Wood. Cambridge: Cambridge University Press, 1998.

— 1783. *Prolegomena to Any Future Metaphysics That Will Be Able to Come Forward As Science, with Kant's Letter to Marcus Herz, February 27, 1772*. Ed. James W Ellington. Indianapolis, IN: Hackett Publishing, 2001.

Kitcher, P. 2002. On the explanatory role of correspondence truth. *Philosophy and Phenomenological Research* 64 (2): 346–64.

Klein, Peter. 2011. Skepticism. In *The Stanford Encyclopedia of Philosophy*. Summer 2011 edn. Ed. Edward N. Zalta.

Korsgaard, C M. 1983. Two distinctions in goodness. *The Philosophical Review* 92 (2): 169–95.

Künne, Wolfgang. 2003. *Conceptions of Truth*. New York: Oxford University Press.

Kvanvig, J. 2008. Pointless truth. *Midwest Studies in Philosophy* 32 (1): 199–212.

Lynch, Michael P. 2001. A functionalist theory of truth. In *The Nature of Truth*. Ed. Michael P. Lynch. Cambridge, MA: MIT Press.

— 2005a. Alethic functionalism and our folk theory of truth. *Synthese* 145 (1): 29–43

— 2005b. *True to Life: Why Truth Matters*. Cambridge, Mass.: MIT Press.

— 2009a. The values of truth and the truth of values. In *Epistemic Value*. Ed. Adrian Haddock, Alan Millar, and Duncan Pritchard. Oxford, UK: Oxford University Press.

— 2009b. *Truth As One and Many*. Oxford; New York : Clarendon Press: Oxford University Press.

MacBride, Fraser. 2013. Truthmakers. In *The Stanford Encyclopedia of Philosophy*. Spring 2013 edn. Ed. Edward N. Zalta.

McGrath, M. 2005. Lynch on the value of truth. *Philosophical Books* 46 (4): 302–10.

Miller, Alexander. 2012. Realism. In *The Stanford Encyclopedia of Philosophy*. Spring 2012 edn. Ed. Edward N. Zalta.

Mulligan, Kevin and Fabrice Correia. 2013. Facts. In *The Stanford Encyclopedia of Philosophy*. Spring 2013 edn. Ed. Edward N. Zalta.

Nozick, R. 1977. *Anarchy, State, and Utopia*. Basic Books.

Park, N., C. Peterson, and M. E. P. Seligman. 2004. Strengths of character and well-being. *Journal of Social and Clinical Psychology* 23 (5): 603–19.

Pears, David. 1951. Universals. *The Philosophical Quarterly* 1 (3): 218.

Pedersen, Nikolaj Jang Lee Linding. 2006. What can the problem of mixed inferences teach us about alethic pluralism? *The Monist* 89 (1): 102–17.

— 2012. Recent work on alethic pluralism. *Analysis* 72 (3): 588–607.

Pedersen, Nikolaj Jang Lee Linding and Cory Wright. 2013. Pluralist theories of truth. In *The Stanford Encyclopedia of Philosophy*. Spring 2013 edn. Ed. Edward N Zalta. http://plato.stanford.edu/archives/spr2013/entries/truth-pluralist/

Peirce, Charles Sanders. 1878. How to make our ideas clear. In *Pragmatism: The Classic Writings*. Ed. H. S. Thayer. Indianapolis, IN: Hackett Publishing, 1982.

Plato. 1997. *Complete Works*. 5th, illustrated edn. Ed. John Madison Cooper and D. S. Hutchinson. Indianapolis, IN: Hackett Publishing.

Priest, Graham. 2006. *Doubt Truth to Be a Liar*. Oxford: Oxford University Press

Putnam, Hilary. 1981. *Reason, Truth, and History*. Cambridge: Cambridge University Press.

Quine, W. V. 1960. *Word and Object*. Cambridge, MA: Technology Press of the Massachusetts Institute of Technology.

— 1970. *Philosophy of Logic*. Englewood Cliffs, NJ: Prentice-Hall.

— 1981. *Theories and Things*. Cambridge, Mass.: Harvard University Press.

— 1992. *Pursuit of Truth*. Cambridge, Mass.: Harvard University Press.

Ramsey, F. P. and G. E. Moore. 1927. Symposium: Facts and propositions. *Proceedings of the Aristotelian Society, Supplementary Volumes* 7: 153–206.

Rodriguez-Pereyra, Gonzalo. 2006. Truthmakers. *Philosophy Compass* 1 (2): 186–200.

Rorty, R. 1995. Is truth a goal of enquiry? Davidson vs. Wright. *The Philosophical Quarterly* 45 (180): 281–300.

Russell, Bertrand. 1906. On the nature of truth. In *Theories of Truth*. Ed. Frederick F. Schmitt. Malden, Mass.: Blackwell, 2003.

— 1912. Truth and falsehood. In *The Nature of Truth: Classic and Contemporary Perspectives*. Ed. Michael P. Lynch. Cambridge, MA: MIT Press, 2001.

Sainsbury, R. M. 1996. Crispin wright: Truth and objectivity. *Philosophy and Phenomenological Research* 56 (4): 899–904.

Salerno, Joe. 2009. *New Essays on the Knowability Paradox*. Oxford: Oxford University Press.

Searle, John R. 1995. *The Construction of Social Reality*. New York: Simon and Schuster.

Shapiro, Stewart. 2009. Michael P. Lynch: Truth as one and many. *Notre Dame Philosophical Reviews*. http://ndpr.nd.edu/news/24169-truth-as-one-and-many/

Sher, Gila. 2005. Functional pluralism. *Philosophical Books* 46 (4): 311–30.

Stich, Stephen P. 1990. *The Fragmentation of Reason: Preface to a Pragmatic Theory of Cognitive Evaluation*. Cambridge, Mass.: MIT Press.

Stoljar, Daniel and Nic Damnjanovic. 2012. The deflationary theory of truth. In *The Stanford Encyclopedia of Philosophy*. Summer 2012 edn. Ed. Edward N Zalta. http://plato.stanford.edu/archives/sum2012/entries/truth-deflationary/

Swoyer, Chris. 2010. Relativism. In *The Stanford Encyclopedia of Philosophy*. Winter 2010 edn. Ed. Edward N. Zalta.

Tappolet, C. 1997. Mixed inferences: A problem for pluralism about truth predicates. *Analysis* 57 (3): 209–10.

Tarski, A. 1944. The semantic conception of truth and the foundations of semantics. *Philosophy and Phenomenological Research* 4 (3): 341–76.

Taylor, Shelley E. 1989. *Positive Illusions: Creative Self-deception and the Healthy Mind*. New York: Basic Books.

Textor, Mark. 2012. States of affairs. In *The Stanford Encyclopedia of Philosophy*. Summer 2012 edn. Ed. Edward N. Zalta.

Warfield, Ted A. and Keith DeRose. 1999. *Skepticism : A Contemporary Reader*. New York: Oxford University Press.

Williamson, Timothy. 1994. A critical study of truth and objectivity. *International Journal of Philosophical Studies* 30 (1): 130–44.

Wittgenstein, Ludwig. 1922. *Tractatus Logico-philosophicus*. Ed. C. K. Ogden. London: Routledge, 1990.

Wrenn, Chase. 2010. True belief is not instrumentally valuable. In *New Waves in Truth*. Ed. C. D. Wright and N. Pedersen. Palgrave Macmillan.

— 2011. Practical success and the nature of truth. *Synthese* 181 (3): 451–70.

Wrenn, Chase B. 2005. Pragmatism, truth, and inquiry. *Contemporary Pragmatism* 2 (1): 95–114.

Wright, Crispin. 1992. *Truth and Objectivity*. Cambridge, Mass.: Harvard University Press.

— 2001. Minimalism, deflationism, pragmatism, pluralism. In *The Nature of Truth*. Ed. Michael P. Lynch. Cambridge, Mass.: MIT Press.

Young, James O. 2013. The coherence theory of truth. In *The Stanford Encyclopedia of Philosophy*. Summer 2013 edn. Ed. Edward N. Zalta.

Index